30-Day Author
DEVELOP A DAILY WRITING HABIT AND WRITE YOUR BOOK IN 30 DAYS (OR LESS)

Kevin Tumlinson

www.happypantsbooks.com

30-DAY AUTHOR
DEVELOP A DAILY WRITING HABIT
AND WRITE YOUR BOOK IN 30 DAYS (OR LESS)

Copyright © 2015 by Kevin Tumlinson
All rights reserved, published by Happy Pants Books

A WORDSLINGER GUIDE
FIRST EDITION: September 2015

ISBN-10: 1530234581
ISBN-13: 978-1530234585

No part of this publication may be reproduced, stored in a retrieval system, or transmitted in any form or by any means, electronic, mechanical, photocopying, recording, or otherwise, without written permission of the publisher. For information regarding permissions, visit http://kevintumlinson.com/contact

ALSO BY KEVIN TUMLINSON

Citadel
Citadel: First Colony
Citadel: Paths in Darkness
Citadel: Children of Light Citadel: Omnibus
Citadel: The Value of War

Sawyer Jackson
Sawyer Jackson and the Long Land
Sawyer Jackson and the Shadow Strait

Wordslinger
30-Day Author: Develop A Daily Writing Habit and Write Your Book In 30 Days (Or Less)

Standalone
Getting Gone
Teresa's Monster
The Three Reasons to Avoid Being Punched in the Face
Tin Man
Two Blocks East
Edge
Evergreen

Watch for more at kevintumlinson.com

FOREWORD
BY HONORÉE CORDER

Until I became an author, I thought writing a book was nearly impossible. One of those mystical and magical achievements only truly special people were able to achieve, such as finishing a marathon or mentally doing complex equations. Then I was encouraged to write my own book and given a few simple instructions to get it done. Within a few weeks, I had completed my first manuscript.

As you'll hear Kevin Tumlinson discuss in the *30-day Author*, very little actual writing time goes into completing a manuscript. You'll find once you get started, the words will flow from your fingers (or lips, if you dictate them).

What takes the most time, and what really slows down an aspiring author's progress, is *thinking* about writing a book. *Marinating* in one's lack of belief in themselves. And, finally, *procrastinating* instead of actually writing.

What I know for certain, seventeen books to my credit later, is that writing a book is possible for just about anyone. Not only because I've done it, but because I see people from different backgrounds, ages, ethnicities, and education levels publish their own books. And not just a few people – lots and lots of them. What do they know that you don't? As it turns out, there's only one real difference between a published author and the person who aspires to be a published author: writing the words. Getting them out of your head and onto the paper or screen is the gap you need to close.

To go one step further, what every published author has in common is the fact that they put in the work to get the book done: *they developed a daily writing habit.*

You see, what you might want to know is the "secret formula" for getting your book finished, and yet there is no secret, and the formula truly consists of one unmistakable and irrefutable action:

You must write, every. single. day.

There are some nuances and distinctions that can, and will, help you, and that's what Kevin Tumlinson's book, the 30-day Author, is going to share with you. You will learn that once you decide to develop a daily writing habit, you, too, will have a book in 30 days. Kevin is fearless in sharing his journey, and generous with his knowledge. His voice is laid-back, almost casual, but make no mistake: what he has to share is pure gold for you.

This is the part where I feel compelled to remind you that 30 days from now will arrive, whether you've put in the time, and written the words, or not. So I encourage you to pull out your calendar, and circle the date 30 days from today. Then finish reading this book, and use the wisdom and lessons contained within to jump-start your writing.

Finally, schedule time every single day to write. The words will pile on top of the other, multiply almost before your eyes, beckoning you to continue. The more you write, the more you'll write … and more you'll *want* to write. Sometimes, all it takes it just getting started. Aren't you ready to get started?

If so, you'll want to take Kevin's formula for getting your first book done, and use it for yourself. I promise that thirty-one days from now you'll be darn glad you did. I certainly hope you do!

To your author success!

Honorée Corder

Author, Prosperity for Writers: A Writer's Guide to Creating Abundance

WHY 30 DAYS?

30 Days.

It just seems like a nice, round number, doesn't it?

It's a benchmark for all kinds of goals, from developing better diet and exercise habits to reading a book to hitting a sales goal. 30 days is a nice, comfortable bucket for people to try to fill.

Now … what about writing a *book* in 30 days?

I've talked to a lot of groups and a lot of will-be authors about this—at live events and book signings, during coaching and consulting calls, and on both the Wordslinger Podcast and the Self Publishing Answers Podcast. And I've gotten a lot of mixed results. Some people are skeptical of the whole thing, and they usually just ignore everything I just said and move along. Obviously, those people probably aren't reading this book.

Some people, however, are really excited by the prospect of taking a book from idea to page in 30 days. They *love* the idea. Because getting a book done *fast* means making it *available* fast. In just 30 days, you could have a book that you can …

>Give as a gift to family and friends
>
>Display on your bookshelf as a mark of accomplishment
>
>Hand to clients to promote and grow your business

Sell for a bit of extra cash, or even as a part of your full-time income

Not bad. Not bad at all.

Most product development cycles take a lot longer than 30 days. Some Apple products have taken *years* to nudge from concept to prototype to final product. I've worked with clients—software developers, for example—who *retire* a product, taking it off the shelves entirely, in less time than it took to develop it in the first place!

The idea of being able to not only write a first draft of a book in 30 days, but possibly even *publish* in 30 days, is a complete fantasy to some people. But for you? It's going to be the new reality.

I'm not just pulling an arbitrary number out of the air here, by the way. I come by the 30-Day Author formula honestly.

My first published book took over two years to write. I squeezed in all the time I thought I could manage, spending long hours in coffee shops and book stores, in sessions spread over months and then years. I wrote from home, when I could work up the energy. When I was a full-time employee at an ad agency, I would sometimes sneak in a bit of writing at work (*shhhh*). I did the whole thing in fits and spurts, until finally, after two long years, I had Book One.

And then I went and promised I'd write another.

So, for two *more* years I trudged along, doing my best to get the ideas on the page in every wee, random hour I could find. I dreaded it all the while. Coming back to that book became a sort of personal nightmare.

And I still had Book Three to write.

I assessed my situation:

I had spent two years writing Book One.

I had delayed more than a year before starting Book Two.

I had spent two years writing Book Two.

I delayed for nearly two years more.

And now ... I *still* had Book Three to write.

This was going to kill me.

Not just finishing the third book in a trilogy, but the whole *process* of writing. I'd been a writer all my life, but this—the writing of books—was so very different from what I knew, and the way I usually worked.

At that point in my life, I was a probably one of the best copywriters in the country.

I'm saying that with absolutely no qualification whatsoever, but I feel pretty confident in it. By that time I'd won awards, I'd pleased a lot of clients, I'd made people a lot of money. I had big names in my portfolio, and big kudos coming from those big names—clients like ExxonMobil, Sysco Foods, Jiffy Lube, HP, and more. I'd even had a video I wrote and produced aired for the President and his cabinet.

So, writing career-wise, I was pretty solid.

And I was *fast*. That copy I was winning awards for? Usually written in just a couple of minutes. Need something longer? Give me the subject, and in an hour or two you'll have a white paper, a case study, a pamphlet, a booklet, a string of blog posts. I could do that, because I had *trained* to do that, all my life.

So why was it that I was only getting small chunks of book out in staggered hours over the course of *years*?

I had to take a hard look at myself, my work process, and my goals.

I wanted a writing career. I mean—I wanted a *book* writing career. And if I was going to have it, I had to get my act together, and I had to figure out the formal process for writing books fast and consistently.

I had to figure out how other authors were doing this, and replicate it.

I remember watching an episode of "Castle," the ABC comedy drama about a crime novelist (played by the incredible Nathan Fillion) who teams up with a New York City police detective (the gorgeous Stana Katic) to solve crimes, ostensibly as an inspiration for his books.

One of the great things about the show, at least early on, was how they would sometimes feature real-world novelists, usually sitting with Castle at a weekly poker game. In one of these episodes, the game includes hyper-prolific author James Patterson. As this group of legendary authors chat and play cards, Patterson says to Castle, "Only one book a year, Rick?" And you can just *hear* the critical judgment in his voice. Castle, of course, reacts with appropriate shame.

That scene summed up for me the whole notion of what it means to be a real, honest to God, writes-a-lot-of-books author:

> If you want to lay claim to the "author" title you have to publish more than a couple of books every few years.

Now ... that's *not true*, of course.

There are certainly *plenty* of authors who *only* publish every few years. Some may only publish one book in their entire *lifetime*. Harper Lee, for example, has two books total—one published in 1949, the other published in 2015. And you'd be hard pressed to find anyone who would refuse to call her an author.

A lot of those "less frequent" authors have accolades galore, and a wealth of adoring readers who absolutely love their work. But that wasn't the kind of author I wanted to be.

I wanted to be the kind of author I grew up reading. I wanted to be an Orson Scott Card, or a Neil Gaiman, or a Stephen King. I wanted to have a whole *shelf* dedicated to my books—maybe even an entire bookcase! I wanted to run my hands along a row of book spines, and touch my name a hundred times or more.

And if I was going to build *that* kind of writing career, I was going to have to get the lead out.

Plus, there was another aspect of my career I had to consider—I wanted to make *money*.

I was kind of delusional on that point for awhile. I had fallen into this sort of fantasy state in which I believed that "if I could *just* get that third book out, people would go *nuts* for it!" My fortune would be made.

Which, it turns out, was not even remotely true.

People *have* gone nuts for those books, but only once they actually *read* them. Before that, they aren't readers, which means they aren't customers. That's because there's another component to being an author that a lot of folks don't like to talk about: Marketing.

People forget about marketing all the time. They forget that people aren't already lined up and waiting for your book to hit shelves. In fact, for most people, it's going to be a pretty disappointing experience if you think that once your book goes on sale you're going to have to fend readers off with a stick. The truth is, if you're not marketing your work, then no one is ever going to know it's there. Unless, of course, you get *incredibly* lucky.

That's a peril for another book, though. Marketing has its own challenges and perks, and those could easily fill volumes. In fact, there are hundreds of books available about marketing your writing. You know ... once you *have* some writing to market.

And that brings us to why we're here.

You can only get a book to market if you actually take the time to write one. By extension, the *faster* you write your book, the faster you can get to marketing it, which leads to all those treasured goals you have. If you want to eventually reach a Patterson level of production, it starts with writing the first book.

Rather than spend two or four or six or more years writing that book, we're going to work on getting you to write it in just 30 days—maybe *less*.

And it's not actually as difficult as you might think.

SPOILER ALERT

The 30-Day Author formula is really pretty simple. It starts with "put butt in chair," followed by "write." Then repeat until you have a book.

See? I just saved you *so much time*. If you're reading this as part of an eBook sample, you just learned the whole process, and you didn't have to pay a dime!

Of course, I'll be expanding on that whole idea a bit in the pages to come. So you might want to stick around. There could be something useful in here.

Oh ... and "why 30 days?"

Because I seriously think people would walk away in disbelief if I called the book "The 15-Day Author." And they'd practically *run* from the book if I called it "The 7-Day Author."

The truth is, you can take the techniques you learn from this book and scale them up and down as needed. Write a book in a week, if that's your thing. Or write it in a year—because there's actually nothing wrong with that. The important part is to actually write, and do it again and again, getting the same great and consistent results each time.

Get into the habit, and repeat that habit every day.

That's what you'll learn in the pages that follow. So let's get started.

WHAT YOU'LL LEARN IN THIS BOOK

This book is broken into two sections:

Part 1: Developing a Daily Writing Habit

In this section, you'll get into the headspace of being an author. You'll learn a few techniques that are meant to help you form a daily writing habit. Learn how to come back to the keyboard or blank page every day, ready to go. Most of the material in this section is "mental game." You should leave Part 1 with the ability to sit down each day and just *start*, without hesitation or writer's block (whatever that is).

Part 2: 30-Day Author Process

This part of the book focuses on more practical aspects of actually writing a book. You'll learn the **30-Day Writing Formula**, which is deceptively simple. You'll also learn techniques for beating writer's block (there's that term again), how to craft an email and a pitch, and even some basic tips on what to do after your book is written. You'll want to bookmark this section so you can come back and reference it from time to time.

Now ... let's roll.

PART 1 – DEVELOPING A DAILY WRITING HABIT

CHAPTER 1
YOU CAN SKIP THIS CHAPTER …

We interrupt this program to bring you a ridiculously important side trail. The following chapter is more inspiration than information. I've put it right here, between a perfectly good introduction and what would have been a perfectly good first chapter.

And the reason is because you may be a lot like me. You may be doing this for all the wrong reasons—at first.

If you have any doubts about why you're doing this, read on. This chapter isn't that long, and you can power through it and maybe learn something in the process.

If you're absolutely *certain* that you're on the right track as an author already, then you can feel free to skip this chapter and go straight to the mechanics of this whole thing. I won't blame you a bit.

CHOOSE YOUR OWN WHY

When I was a kid, I used to love to read "Choose Your Own Adventure" novels. And I admit, I was sort of a cheater with them. Because I was always curious what that other road might have been like. So I'd make my choice, and read the result, but then I'd quickly thumb back and read the *other* choice, to see what might have been.

I've always been fascinated with alternate realities—it's even a running theme in my novels.

But who knew that those books would be good practice for a future in writing? Because (and I swear it's true), sometimes it feels exactly like I'm living in a Choose Your Own Adventure book.

Do I work on Book A or Book B?

Do I take on this client, who might soak up a lot of my time (but pay a nice check), or do I focus instead on marketing an upcoming release?

Do I pay an editor or hand my book to beta readers?

Those are just some of the questions I ask myself almost every day. But there's one question I only had to ask myself *once*. And the answer changed everything:

What's my why?

That's the million-dollar question, because the answer is at the heart of everything you do from here out.

For example:

Why do I have to get up at 4 AM every morning? Because of my *why*.

Why do I have to read all of this research? Because of my *why*.

Why do I have to go to this conference? Because of my *why*.

Sounds kind of silly when I read it back, but it's actually kind of profound. There are a lot of daily choices in my life that would make no sense whatsoever if my *why*. was different.

So what is my *why*?

> I want to be a prolific and prosperous author of hopeful, fun, and inspiring stories.

That's it. That's the whole *why* behind everything I do. I want *that*, so I do *this*. Or *that*. Or the *other thing*. A *lot* of the other thing.

My *why* drives every decision, every choice, every allocation of funds or time or resources. My *why* has caused me to let some friendships slide while building new friendships that make more sense for my life. It's caused me to make lifestyle decisions that virtually make me a different person than I was a year or two earlier. It drives me to do things that would have made no sense before, but are perfectly in tune with my goals now. The *Why* is life.

So what's *your* why?

Why do you want to be an author? Or why do you think you'll be able to stick out long, tedious hours of writing or editing or waiting for your readers to leave comments? What is it about this work that appeals to you enough to dedicate yourself to it? What in the world is your *why*?

I'll be honest, I wasn't always crystal clear on my *why* for a really long time. In fact, I let things get kind of muddy for a while there. This book, actually, was tied up in a path I was taking, for a time, that wasn't really a good fit for my *why*. Which is how it came to be shelved for most of a year while I got myself back on track.

I became clear on my *why* when I went to a writer's conference in Austin, Texas, in April of 2015. The conference was the Sterling & Stone Colony Summit, and it was a sort of sequel to another gathering that I'd missed out on the year before.

Everyone attending this summit was an indie author. And every one of us paid quite a big chunk of money to be there. Big, at least, for me. At the time, I had exactly $0 in book sales, on a recurring basis. Which, if you're any good at math, adds up to *not making a living*.

I was making my living entirely from client work. Writing books, at that point, was something I was passionate about and dedicated to, but not something I'd really given myself over to completely. Not yet.

Oh, I *thought* had. For most of a year prior to the Summit, I had been working on the business side of my author career. I had written a few books by then, and I was dabbling in the marketing side. I'd met and teamed up with my writing and business partner, Nick Thacker. I had tried, again and again, to launch something I thought might give us enough residual income to support us as we wrote books, but that just wasn't happening fast enough. Basically, for most of the year I was learning as I went. But I wasn't making much progress.

When I decided I would go to the summit, and I forked over my cash, I had this idea that I was going to learn how to improve my *non-fiction* business. Which, as it turned out, was more of a *non-book* business.

I was struggling to cut ties with clients, and to do that I figured I'd better do something that had a big chance of pulling in some quick cash. So I was spending all my time and energy trying to write non-fiction books, trying to develop courses, trying to build up a coaching business, and essentially doing everything *but* the work I really *wanted* to do. I had, in effect, fallen into the same pit I've fallen into a thousand times over the course of my career:

> "I'll just do X until it takes off and pays for my living, and then I'll start writing fiction."

I was *always* doing that—deferring what I *really* wanted in favor of doing something else, hoping it would pay off big and give me the freedom to go do the first thing I wanted. Kind of silly, actually. It's a terrible way to pursue a dream. The dream itself is always just out of reach, because you're the one *pushing* it out of reach.

This was exactly what I was doing—*again*—when I attended the Summit. I was thinking in terms of building a business around the non-fiction work, and I was going to use my "hot seat" in front of the whole group to get the advice I thought I needed to make things break over.

But when I sat in that chair, and faced Sean Platt and Johnny B. Truant and the rest of the gathered writers and publishers in that room, it hit me ...

I was asking all the wrong questions.

Everyone else was asking about how to market their books, or how to write better or faster, or how to finish a difficult project.

Some asked for advice on developing a writing habit, but more often they asked about how to bump their book sales to the *next level*.

It hit me, sitting there, that the majority of people in that room were already doing the one thing I kept *saying* I wanted to do, but was somehow always *refusing* to do. They were making their *living* by writing and selling *books*.

I sputtered through my hot seat, and got the kind of answers you might expect from a room full of people who are on to your shenanigans. No one in that room believed that my plans were a good idea, because it was pretty plain that what I *really* wanted was to be a *fiction author*.

After my hot seat, my head was spinning. I started thinking about everything that was going on all around me, about the excited conversations and the sudden sparks of enthusiasm for a new marketing idea or a new book idea or a new series idea. Somehow I had managed to alienate myself from all of those conversations. Because, unlike everyone else in the room, I wasn't working toward my *why*.

I was working *against* it.

That's why I have temporarily diverted you from the pure path of learning how to write a book in 30 days. I want to reach out to you, to help you get this really big, really important concept into your head and into your heart:

Figure out your why.

And when you do, make sure that every single thing you do, from here on out, is done for your *why*, and for *no other reason*.

Neil Gaiman, author of "American Gods," among many other great books, gave a commencement speech at the University of the Arts, in which he summed up his why by comparing it to a mountain—

Something that worked for me was imagining that where I wanted to be—

an author, primarily of fiction, making good books, making good comics and supporting myself through my words – was a mountain. A distant mountain. My goal.

And I knew that as long as I kept walking towards the mountain I would be all right. And when I truly was not sure what to do, I could stop, and think about whether it was taking me towards or away from the mountain. I said no to editorial jobs on magazines, proper jobs that would have paid proper money because I knew that, attractive though they were, for me they would have been walking away from the mountain. And if those job offers had come along earlier I might have taken them, because they still would have been closer to the mountain than I was at the time.

Watch this whole commencement here: http://www.uarts.edu/neil-gaiman-keynote-address-2012 (totally worth it)

Sitting there at the Colony Summit, with all those people offering me heartfelt wisdom, I was sick to discover that I had been inadvertently walking away from my mountain, while thinking I was moving toward it all the while. So, when my hot seat was done and I took my boring old *normal* seat again, I began rethinking everything.

I thought about what it was that I really *wanted* to do, and I decided that, money be damned, I was going to *do it*. I was going to be a fiction author *first*, and everything else *second*—and I'd only do what it took to reached my mountain.

I left the summit early that day (something I kind of regret now, but at the time seemed the best plan). I drove from Austin to Houston, about three hours, in total silence. I prayed, because that's a big part of my life too. And I asked God what he thought about this whole thing, and about what I was doing and where I was at the time.

My decision, made long before I rolled into my driveway and made my way wearily inside, was that I would write more books. And more books. And more. Until the world was just *filled* with my fiction. Because that would get me closer to the mountain than ever.

That's it. That's the whole thing. I wanted to share it before we went any further, in case it could inspire you or make you think about why you're here. Because why you're here *matters*. It may be the *only* thing that matters.

Now we can get to the real meat of this book—the important bits that will help you move toward your own *why*, your own mountain.

And we'll start by building a brand new habit.

CHAPTER 2
WRITING IS HARD

Writing is hard.

You know it. I know it. There's no point beating around the bush about it. Writing is the chore you've always dreaded, even though you knew it was good for you. Like eating broccoli. You might choke it down, but it's much tougher to learn to *love* it.

(Honestly, what *is it* with broccoli? It's like eating tiny little trees, right?)

When I talk to people who are struggling to get into writing full time, the biggest challenge is always the **daily writing habit**.

It's tough to develop the discipline to sit down every day and put hands on a keyboard. It's a struggle just to start.

Early in my career I was a teacher, putting a Masters of Education and a state teaching certification to work in classrooms at public and private schools, and then on college campuses. Later, I became a coach and a consultant, teaching people how to be better writers, how to start a business around this stuff, and how to use writing to improve their lives and their careers. I also became the host of the Wordslinger Podcast, and co-host of the Self Publishing Answers Podcast—both of which have been great opportunities to talk to other authors, and share what I've learned.

So I've done a lot of teaching on this subject, and in that I've tried to help people develop the discipline to do this stuff every day.

When I'm teaching someone to do something difficult, I like to start with the very root, the most basic element, the ground zero of the whole thing. And ground zero for discipline is **commitment.**

The thing is, the fact that you want to write *better* and write *more* doesn't make you unique. Lots of people have the same goal. But getting to that goal is like getting to six-pack abs. It takes more than just wishing for it really hard. Trust me—I've wished for a six-pack for years, and remain "robust." Chicken wings, man.

What it takes to develop a daily writing habit, just like getting into shape, is commitment to doing the work. And because writing is hard, it takes a commitment to causing ourselves a bit of pain and discomfort.

> "I'm continually trying to make choices that put me against my own comfort zone. As long as you're uncomfortable, it means you're growing."
>
> —Ashton Kutcher

Thanks Ashton Kutcher. Your wise words illustrate my point *beautifully.*

Because that discomfort isn't going to go away for a long, *long* time. It's something you'll have to learn to live with until you've mastered the discipline of daily writing.

So, now that you know you're going to be a wee bit uncomfortable, let's start by making the following statement:

Today, I commit to ...

... fill in the blank.

"Today I commit to writing one blog post." Or "Today I commit to writing 1,000 words." Or maybe, "Today I commit to writing one autoresponder email."

You can commit to more, or you can commit to less. The quantity doesn't matter right now. What *does* matter is that you are making a verbal, out-loud, no-takesy-backsies *pledge* with yourself to *do something.*

This may seem trivial and unimportant, but the truth is when we say something out loud it carries a lot of weight with us, psychologically speaking. It *means* something. We subconsciously want to make something we tell ourselves into the *truth*, because we already made it a part of our *reality* by saying it out loud.

Here's the deal: Writers are in the business of making thoughts into things. We take ideas and we put them on the page. They go from some sort of abstract energy construct floating in our gray matter to being little black letters on a white background. Words *mean* something. Words are *things*. So when we say words out loud, we're adding something to reality. Get it?

Our brains simply do not like having to accept something that isn't true. When we say something that we know to be a lie, there are consequences both psychological and physiological.

Ever told a fib and gotten that little twinge in your gut? Ever felt your heart sink after you told a little white lie? Ever felt like throwing up after spinning a whopper of a yarn? Your body is responding to what your brain knows is an out-an-out falsehood. We call this "cognitive dissonance," and it's responsible for most of the stress that people feel today.

> *In psychology, cognitive dissonance is the mental stress or discomfort experienced by an individual who holds two or more contradictory beliefs, ideas, or values at the same time, or is confronted by new information that conflicts with existing beliefs, ideas, or values.*
>
> *[Wikipedia, https://en.wikipedia.org/wiki/Cognitive_dissonance Retrieved 23 September 2015]*

We humans really don't like to lie to ourselves. It upsets our tummies, among other things.

In fact, **PRO TIP**:

> If you're feeling anxiety or stress in your daily life, take a look at the stories you're telling yourself, and ask yourself if there's anything there that you don't really believe, or don't really want to believe. It'll do wonders for your health.

So, cognitive dissonance is bad. And to avoid cognitive dissonance, we will often do whatever it takes to make our self-talk true. And we writers and will-be authors can use that to our advantage.

Making this commitment is about deciding to develop a *discipline*, and then taking small actions to make that discipline a reality. This is a simple first step, but it's an important one. So say it.

"Today I commit to …"

Fill in the blank at the end of that sentence.

And then do it.

CHAPTER 3
DAILY AFFIRMATIONS

You may have heard about affirmations in the past. They sometimes have—well, we'll say an *unfortunate* reputation.

Meaning they get kind of a bum wrap. They end up being bundled in with this faux-new-agey idea that just repeating a phrase to yourself several times a day will magically make what you want appear out of nowhere.

Tell yourself you're rich, and money will appear. Tell yourself you're thin, and the pounds will just melt off. Tell yourself you're a successful author, and books will magically write themselves and readers will be drawn to you like flies to honey.

Repetitive wishing.

I think that the reputation for affirmations is unfortunate, because affirmations are about *so much more* than *wishing*. There's actually research that suggests that writing or saying an affirmation every day can create the chemical and neural pathways in your brain to make it a permanent part of *who you are*.

In 1985, Michael F. Scheier and Charles S. Carver published a study titled "Optimism, Coping, and Health: Assessment and Implications of Generalized Outcome Expectancies." In that study they analyzed the impact of both optimism and pessimism on problem solving ability.

In a 2012 Atlantic article, Michael Scheier is quoted saying:

> *"We know why optimists do better than pessimists. Optimists are not simply being Pollyannas; they're problem solvers who try to improve the situation."*

SOURCE:
http://www.theatlantic.com/health/archive/2012/04/how-the-power-of-positive-thinking-won-scientific-credibility/256223/

Participants in the study used positive affirmations to boost their self confidence, improve their outlook, and ultimately overcome obstacles in pursuit of their goals.

Affirmations can be a delicious part of your complete breakfast—an exercise in telling yourself, over and again, what you most want to be, and tuning your brain to start doing what it takes to get there.

The truth is loads of successful people use daily affirmations as a warm-up to their day, and to help them get their brain focused on doing things that lead to their goals.

Scott Adams, the cartoonist and writer behind the *Dilbert* comic strip, talks about daily affirmations in his book, *How to Fail at Almost Everything and Still Win Big*.

> *Affirmations are simply the practice of repeating to yourself what you want to achieve while imagining the outcome you want. You can write it, speak it, or just think it in sentence form. The typical form of an affirmation would be "I, Scott Adams, will become an astronaut." The details of affirmations probably don't matter much because the process is about improving your focus, not summoning magic.*

Adams, Scott (2013-10-22). How to Fail at Almost Everything and Still Win Big: Kind of the Story of My Life (p. 154). Penguin Group US. Kindle Edition.

He goes on to say—

> *When you practice affirmations and you happen to succeed in the area of your focus, it feels like extraordinary luck. That's how you perceive it, anyway. The Dilbert success story is engorged with lucky-sounding events.*
>
> *Adams, Scott (2013-10-22). How to Fail at Almost Everything and Still Win Big: Kind of the Story of My Life (p. 158). Penguin Group US. Kindle Edition.*

So ... not magic. And not luck, either.

Instead, affirmations are like a program you install in your brain to keep you alert for possibilities, keep you focused on productive tasks, and keep you working toward the achievement of your goals.

I used to write long, elaborate descriptions of my goals and what I wanted for my life. I'd spend hours crafting them, breaking them out into bullet points of benchmarks and waypoints. And when it was all said and done, I had some nicely written goals, suitable for any of your better business books or self-help seminars.

And yet, I hardly ever achieved those goals.

The problem, at least for me, was that I wasn't actually *paying attention* to the things I'd written. The documents I was creating were so hefty and detailed, I never felt like looking back and observing what I'd had in mind. I had elaborate goals, but I wasn't following the plans I'd laid out. Because those plans were just too heavy. Too bulky. Reading that, even once a week, was going to soak up time I didn't have—or, to be more accurate, time I wasn't willing to give—time I could spend on actually *producing* something.

Affirmations are a shortcut to that whole goal-writing, goal-checking process.

By writing out a simple goal, and repeating it to yourself every day, you're hacking your brain, getting it focused on what's important, and ignoring what isn't.

I had used affirmations before reading Scott's book, but the simplicity of what he was doing really hit home for me. I've modified it a bit, giving it some "rules" I follow, and which seem to work for me.

Here's an example of one of my own affirmations:

I, Kevin Tumlinson, am a wealthy and successful full-time author.

Simple, right? But that one affirmation took *months* to craft. In fact, to this day I still tinker with it. I sometimes substitute "novelist" for "author." I go back and forth on whether I should use "wealthy" or "prosperous" or "affluent."

Words matter, remember?

Regardless, you can see that the current iteration of my affirmation is infinitely more nuanced than where it started:

I will be a wealthy author.

That one is shorter, obviously, but also less focused. It was also projecting into the future, instead of claiming the goal for *right now*. It was originally focused more on who I *would be* rater than *who I am*.

So I tinkered with it to get it to exactly what I wanted it to be, and I started writing it fifteen times a day, every single day.

The effect of that has been *amazing*. Because in many respects, I am exactly the author I describe in that affirmation.

I may not be able to buy a private island, but I do enjoy a certain level of wealth from my work. And successful ... well, I defined both wealth and success as part of this process, and I've met both of those definitions. I'm a full-time author, and I have the life I set out to achieve. Now I'm working toward a new set of goals, and a new set of definitions, and that's the whole point.

Actually—come to think of it, no ... it isn't the point after all.

The *whole* point involves more of a "why" for writing daily affirmations. I had to define for myself the reason I was doing this, so that I could mentally justify the work. I needed something that would explain to my brain, in simple terms, the best possible reasons to write these things every day rather than use that time to do something else.

And here it is:

> *Writing something every day is better than writing nothing every day—and writing something affirming every day is better than writing something pointless.*

We're here to learn how to develop a daily writing habit, and that means developing certain core disciplines. Chief among those—**sit your butt in a chair and *write*.**

And if you're going to do that, you might as well write something that benefits you and produces *meaning* for you.

This is a practice, to develop a habit, and not the sort of writing you'll do full time. But as a practice, it's *incredibly* beneficial.

For starters, it takes the sting out of having to figure out "what to write."

Have you ever sat down with the best of intentions, and faced the blinking cursor or the blank page, and just *froze*? The spirit was willing, but the flesh was weak.

If you do not yet have the habit of sitting down to the page, engaging your brain and shifting into writer mode, and just *getting to it*, then you will often freeze up, waiting for something to jar you loose. And that's what affirmations for the 30-Day Author are all about. They're one-part "confidence building" and one part "motor priming."

Affirmations help you get past the "blank page freeze" because, all else aside, you know you're going to sit down and write *something*. It takes the pressure off.

And *how* your write your affirmations doesn't really matter. You can write them by hand in a Moleskine notebook, using a fancy fountain pen, if that's your thing. Or you can write them using your laptop and a word processor. It doesn't matter what tools you use—your goal is to acclimate yourself and develop a habit of sitting down and *writing*, every single day, without fail.

Affirmations are one of the first things I recommend to will-be authors because they have such a positive impact on your mental game, while also helping you to develop some daily writing muscle memory. Even after you get into the groove and start writing regularly, I recommend you keep up the practice of a daily affirmation. It's just a good, clean habit to have. And a good reminder of your goals. And that's always something worth doing.

Let's take a look at some rules you can use to help you create your affirmations.

8 RULES FOR CREATING YOUR DAILY AFFIRMATION

Write in first person—"I" is powerful. It's *you*, owning what you're saying. If you want to create a new idea of yourself, and live that idea, you should always start at "I."

Use your name—It's a bit redundant, but when we make "contracts" with people we use this format. And this is a contract you have with *you*. So make it official, and name all the parties involved (there's just the one, so it won't take long).

Be specific—Don't just say, "I, Joe Smith, will be rich." Elaborate a bit on *how* you'll "be rich," and what being rich *means* to you. You can do this in shorthand, and I'll explain how to fold in layers of meaning for this in a moment.

Be present—Claim this *right now*, not in some amorphous future. Define your reality a bit. "I am" is a powerful signal to your brain. Claim it, own it, be it.

Write it 10 to 15 times per day—It doesn't matter how. Write it by hand or use a word processor. I have a file in Scrivener (a great piece of organizational and writing software) that has all my affirmations as well as my daily journal. I also have old notebooks where I wrote by hand, when I didn't have a computer handy. You might write your affirmations using Evernote or Microsoft Word or maybe just a pad of Post-It notes. The important part is to develop the daily habit of writing, and the habit of thinking of yourself as an author.

Write it before writing—I write in the mornings. You may write at night. *When* you write doesn't matter as much as the writing itself. But before you put a word on the page for your book or anything else, write your affirmations. They're a trigger to your brain saying "this is writing time." This really helps reduce "writer's block" (whatever that is—we'll talk about it later).

Define each term—Once you have your affirmation written, start a separate document and write definitions for every term you've used. Define "wealth" and "success" and even "author" (if you used those terms) exactly the way you *mean* them. In other words, define what those terms mean to *you*, not just what the dictionary tells you they mean. Get clear in your head exactly what it means for you to have what you're affirming. You can even define related terms that aren't included in the affirmation, such as "book" or "money" or "time." This is where you can go word crazy, and pontificate endlessly. You need never look at this list again, as long as you know, instinctively, what you mean by every word of your affirmation.

Refine as you go—Like I said, I started with one affirmation, and refined it over time. Don't worry if yours isn't perfect. If you write this for a week or a month and decide it could be fine-tuned or refined, do it. Always keep refining, until your affirmation represents your real goals and ambitions as an author.

CHAPTER 4
DAILY BLOG

Affirmations are a great warm-up to daily writing because they get you focused on the end goal as well as the task at hand. If you did nothing else to develop a daily writing habit, I'd recommend this one exercise.

But getting yourself into the habit of putting words on the page, every single day, can have more *practical* applications, too.

Part of the author's job (whether traditionally published or as an indie publisher) is marketing and promoting their work. Your goal is to build a **platform**—a framework that allows you to consistently reach your target audience *where they are*, and give them something of value in return for their attention.

A good tool for extending your platform and your reach is to engage in **content marketing**. This is the practice of producing and providing content that engages your existing audience while encouraging audience growth. In other words, content marketing is all about giving something of value to your readers, so they will continue to support you and help you grow your author business, doing quirky little things like buying your books.

One of the most common and effective tools used in a content marketing strategy is a **blog**.

You probably read dozens of blogs, and may follow a few

regularly. These are simple websites that let the writer go straight to his or her audience with relevant and engaging content.

You can blog on any topic you like—from deeply personal to purely professional—and publish it easily. There are hundreds of blogging platforms that let you reach your audience for free, including WordPress, Blogger, and Wix.

Having a blog comes with multiple advantages. Here are just a few—

Instant online platform—If you don't already have a website, starting a blog gives you one right away. Your platform can grow from nothing to online in just a few minutes, and just by answering a few simple questions. This web presence is a vital part of your author platform, so it's a *must* to have a website. Blogs are the fastest shortcut to that, and you can always upgrade to a more elaborate site (that *includes* the blog!) later.

Discoverability and search engine optimization (SEO)—Now that you have a web presence, you'll be a lot easier to find. Readers may not come rushing to your digital door just because you have a blog, but as you devote time to creating content it will become easier for readers to stumble across you, whereas they may never have noticed you before. Creating regularly updated content (daily, in this case) on a blog means generating words that can be crawled and indexed by search engines, such as Google. As you write more, you'll see more benefits from search engine optimization, or SEO. In a nutshell, this means that your content is easier to find when people search for specific terms. It increases the chances of *organic traffic*, or people coming to your website because they found you in a search. Daily, relevant content makes you a wider search target, and gets you more hits.

Build a relationship with your readers—You may not have considered this, but authors need one thing more than any other, if they intend to keep being authors: **Authors need *readers*.** And readers are, by some strange reports, actually *human beings.* And thanks to my personal research (such as parties, gatherings, and soirees), I've discovered people like to interact with other people. Having a blog where people can read your content and comment on it means opening the door to this two-way communication and interaction. It allows you to build a relationship with your readers that could lead to book sales, among other perks. Keeping regularly updated content on your blog means that you're encouraging regular engagement with readers, and that is always a good thing.

Build a daily writing habit—And, of course, the biggest benefit for you, as a budding author, is that writing a daily blog post is a good way to get into the habit of writing *every day*. The mere act of sitting down in front of your screen and getting your brain engaged in the process of writing every day is like getting up, lacing on your sneakers, and going for a run. It's conditioning, and it pays exponential, ever-increasing dividends the more you habituate it into your life.

You probably noticed the "daily post" mentions above. Don't panic. Your blog doesn't have to be *epic* or even *elaborate* for it to be *effective*. It's more important that it be *consistent* and *focused*.

Choose a topic that works for you—your journey as an author, maybe, or your love of knitting or your obsession with '80s rock bands—it should be relevant to the topic you plan to write books about. Write a paragraph or two on the topic every day. If some days you feel like you can really kick it out and write more, then write more. If some days all you can manage is a paragraph or two, write that. The point of your blog, at least for *this* program, is to get you into the daily, consistent habit of writing.

If you decide at some point that you'd like to leverage your blog as a marketing tool, or even try to make it a revenue stream, you at least have a solid start for it with all this daily writing.

You're welcome, future you.

DAILY BLOG STARTERS

Having trouble figuring out what to write each day? Here's a list I often give out when I'm consulting or speaking about the 30-Day Author program. Use these daily starters as a guide. You can aim to write about each of these in turn, or just pick and choose the topics you like best. They're just a quick guide, and totally optional.

If you'd like a handy, printable graphic of these starters, you can download one from kevintumlinson.com/resources.

Sunday: Inspiration — Places you've visited (or want to visit), books you've read, people you've admired

Monday: Humor — The cat videos you've seen, a movie you watched, a joke you heard, a funny article you read

Tuesday: Social — People in your life, someone you saw at the coffee shop, a friend you had growing up

Wednesday: Current Events — Something from the news, something from your personal life, something from Facebook

Thursday: Acts of Kindness — Something remembered, something you want to do, a charity you love

Friday: Behind the Curtain — Your process, or the process of another writer, how something works

Saturday: Deep Dive — A topic you're passionate about, something you always wanted to know

CHAPTER 5
DAILY JOURNAL

Some people aren't comfortable with the idea of blogging and putting their thoughts on the interwebz every day, especially if their topic of choice is something personal.

I think this is an odd hang-up for someone who wants to be an author, but I respect it. The story we show to the public can be shaped and cultivated and curated to be exactly what we want or need it to be. We may not always want to share our raw, personal perspective.

In that case, you can get many of the same benefits of blogging just by keeping a **daily journal**. You lose the audience building aspects, and the discoverability and marketing muscle, but daily journaling can be a very cathartic and rewarding experience that can help you grow as an author.

I have a blog, but I also keep a daily journal. It's a habit I started as far back as second grade, when I bought a "Diary" from Scholastic Books, and essentially started filling in the blanks of the writing prompts inside. After that, I had a recurring habit of getting my hands on notebooks and filling them with entries from my day-to-day. I still have all of those journals, and I cherish them. They give me a pretty unique insight into who I was at any given time in my life.

Journals are a great way to develop the daily writing habit because they're unfiltered and easy to produce. People tend to be a lot less "uptight" about what goes into a journal, assuming that they'll be the only one who ever sees it. So for fifteen minutes to half an hour, you can write without worry, and keep your inner editor switched off.

This is perfect for warming up before tackling the writing you'll need to do for your book. It gets you in the right headspace (i.e. "I'm *writing*" vs "I *want* to write"), and helps you feel comfortable with the idea of putting words on the page.

I journal in the mornings, but you can use any time that works best for you. My recommendation is to do it just prior to your "work" writing, though. Writing a quick journal entry helps you warm up, and to build and sustain the momentum you need to knock out a daily word target (more on this later).

You should also aim to write for no more than 15 to 30 minutes (and in fact, 15 minutes would be best). You can always come back to the journal later, to make an entry more elaborate or to add more to it. But as a warm-up, try to keep it to a quick bit of writing, maybe 15-minutes or less. Your goal is to build the habit and reflex of writing daily, and then get into more productive writing to make progress on your book or whatever copywriting you need to do.

If, however, it turns out that you have plenty of time, and that you are consistent with meeting your daily word target, even with a lengthy journal entry, then by all means, journal away! You'll find it to be one of the best motivational tools in your bag, and it's amazing how useful it can be to look back at past entries when you're further down the road. You may find inspiration, themes to explore, characters to develop, or story ideas, all buried within the pages of your journal.

Below is a format I use for my journal entries. You can use this, or modify it to taste, but I do recommend keeping each entry tagged with both the date and the time. It helps with tracking your progress, among other things. But it's also good for "score keeping." You can easily track which days you skipped. And since your goal is to skip *zero* days, tracking your writing times will allow you to guilt yourself into writing more consistently.

Guilt—the time-honored tool of writers throughout history.

Now, the format:

Monday, 19 June 2015

5:00 AM

Yesterday I went to the flea market with Bob, and it was a gorgeous day! The weather was perfect—about 65*F all day, but with the sun it felt comfortable, even in a T-shirt.

We found some great bargains, and I picked up an old 1950s radio that I'll clean up and use as a conversation piece in my office. I also found an old portable Royal typewriter that was in perfect condition, and even included a carrying case! I was thinking of cleaning that up and even taking it to Starbucks, where I can get a little attention and a few smiles from people watching me. Maybe I can hand out cards and encourage people to buy my books.

I'm thinking of sticking an Apple sticker on the back of this thing.

See? Nothing difficult about that. In fact, it's pretty much the easiest kind of writing because you're mostly reporting what you've done and how you feel about it. You can turn off your inner editor and just *write*.

Doing that every day will build in the muscle memory and reflexes you need to tackle other writing projects, so grab a journal or open a file on your computer and get started.

The bonus is you'll have a record of your progress in both life and career, so you can look back from the future and smile at who you once were.

CHAPTER 6
EMAILS & AUTORESPONDERS

Earlier we talked about content marketing, and using blogs to make yourself more discoverable, or to help in building your author platform and even marketing your work. Content marketing is a powerful tool, and exploring it fully goes way beyond the scope of this book. But blogging is a good first step in developing content that can benefit you down the road.

Another powerful tool is email.

I want to start this with a tip, and it's one you really, *really* need to pay attention to:

> You need a mailing list.

Actually, if you're in this game for more than a few minutes, you're probably going to hear that advice again, and again, and again (and again). That's because the mailing list is *still* the most powerful marketing tool any of us has. It gives us an audience of people to market to directly, and (if the list was built right), they're all targeted and qualified as readers of your work.

One of my biggest frustrations, when I first started my author business, was that no one would tell me *how* to build a mailing list.

Any advice I got seemed tantamount to, "Um … well… you wish *really, really hard*." Not helpful.

I can't give you a full course on building a list, because there are just too many options to explore, and too many directions you can go. Maybe in the not-tool-distant future I'll create something that shares a bit of insight into building a mailing list.

For now, though, I can only offer a few basic tips:

Sign up for a mail service such as Aweber or Constant Contact. I actually recommend Author.Email (or authoremail.com if you prefer old-school URLs!). I recommend it for three reasons: I'm one of the founders of it (full disclosure), it's incredibly inexpensive (even free under 1,000 subscribers), and it's really, *really* good. But regardless of the service you choose, make sure it will accommodate your needs and that it will grow with you as you improve your marketing.

Put an opt-in on your website. An "opt-in" basically just means a signup box, where site visitors can register to be on your mailing list. You'll want it to be easy to find. In fact, make it impossible *not* to find. Put it at the end of every blog post, and on every single page of the site, with a call-to-action (CTA) to the effect of "Register to get a free book!" or similar. If you don't have a free book, offer something else, like a short story or some other special, can't-find-it-anywhere-else giveaway. This is what's sometimes called a "lead magnet," and it's basically just a freebie used to entice people to get into your marketing funnel.

Ask your friends and family to opt-in. DO NOT opt them in on your own. Trust me on this. It seems like everyone you know would be thrilled to be on your mailing list, but that isn't always the case. Some people really resent it. So ask. Get their permission. And then add them.

Write lots of good content. And don't just limit it to your blog. Go write content for other blogs, too. Write free articles for other sites. Write book reviews. Write interviews you've conducted with others. This can be a great way to keep building your daily writing habit while also generating lots of points of contact. And at the end of everything you write, include your bio, along with a CTA that says something like, "Get a free book/PDF/short story at yourdomain.com/register."

Building a list takes a while, so the sooner you start the better. But trust me, it's worth every second and every effort.

A mailing list is the single most valuable marketing tool you'll create for your author business. It lets you reach your audience regularly, delivering new content, news about your work, announcements, promotions and giveaways, and just a "howdy do" to keep your audience engaged.

That said, once you have your list, you'll need to email them regularly. And that necessity can be a perfect way to get your author muscles bulked up.

First, let's make a point:

> *Every* email you ever write is a good opportunity to hone and improve your writing skills.

You should treat every email—personal or otherwise—as a good place to practice. In fact, personal emails are perfect for not only improving grammar and mechanics, but also improving your overall writing skills and honing your voice. They're a safe place to experiment, to see what works. You can stretch your legs a bit, try a few things that might seem over the top, without worrying too much about crashing and burning in front of someone who can control your financial future.

Beyond just honing your craft and skill, however, what you'll want to develop in your daily writing habit is *structure* and *organization*. And a good way to do that is with an **email series**.

Have you ever signed up for someone's newsletter and started seeing daily emails that guide you through a multi-step program, or introduce you to new ideas or new resources? Over the course of a week or sometimes a month (or more, in some cases) you may get an email every day. This series may have been the reason you signed up in the first place. Maybe you were lured in by something along the lines of "Join the list and get my FREE 8-Day series about wealth generation!"

Those emails were pre-written, obviously, and timed to release each day after you join the list. This is called an **autoresponder series**, and the goal is to build a relationship with the reader, and to provide them with value in exchange for being a member of your community. These emails are also meant to encourage readers to take a specific action. It is a form of automated engagement that is a common practice in marketing, and one you'll want to be very familiar with.

If you want to see an example of an autoresponder in action, feel free to sign up for mine, and get some free books while you're at it. Go to http://kevintumlinson.com/starterlibrary and sign up. You'll get a link to three free books, and you'll start getting my autoresponder series that feeds out over several days. You can unsubscribe any time, but I encourage you to wait out the entire email series, and maybe wait for a few of my "list pings," with announcements and offers. It will let you see exactly how this can work.

And, you know, you'll be supporting this handsome and lovable Wordslinger while you're at it. So ... bonus.

An autoresponder series is a great way to introduce new readers to who you are and what you're doing. Those emails require time to write—so why not kill two birds with one daily writing habit?

Make an autoresponder series part of your daily warm up.

Choose a topic that will relate to your work. If you are a public speaker, your email series can focus on one of the topics of your talks. If you speak about exercise and fitness, for example, you could create an autoresponder series that offers 5 steps for exercising at the office. Your offer for joining your mailing list might say, "Join my mailing list and get a free 5-day course on staying fit in the workplace!" That's a topic that ties in well with your business, and it provides value for the reader while keeping you front and center in their inbox.

Now that you have your topic, it's time to start writing those emails.

I use Evernote to do this work, but you can use any word processor or text editor for the task. I like Evernote because it allows me to keep an entire series of emails in one place, to access them from any device (laptops, phones, tablets, etc.) to make quick edits or do a quick cut-and-paste, and it's easily shareable, so my business partner and I can both add to or edit the work.

My advice is to create a folder where your emails will live until you're ready to use them, and write each email as a separate document, named for its part in the series. This is simple in Evernote, but for a word processor (such as Microsoft Word), you might consider creating an actual folder named for your email series, and then creating individual Word documents for each email.

For example, if you're using Scrivener, you might create a file called "5-Day Workplace Fitness - Email Autoresponder," and save that in a folder called "Autoresponders" on your hard drive. In Scrivener, you would then create files for each day of the series, and for each of those files you'd write a unique email that outlines a fitness step, and includes a **call to action (CTA)**.

A CTA is just a behavior you want your reader to engage in. You might ask people in this fitness series to buy your book, for example, or contact you to book you for a speaking engagement or to get some coaching.

Using this series as part of your daily warm-up has the side benefit of giving you marketing materials you can use later. Don't worry if your CTA needs to change, down the road. No one needs to even see these emails until you're ready. You can always go back and update them, as needed. But they're going to prove invaluable later on, and you'll be thanking yourself for writing them ahead of time, before the really hectic stuff starts.

Beyond email series, though, you can use email writing as a warm up in other useful ways. Write emails to people you'd like to interview for your book, or to organizations where you'd like to speak, or to former clients to ask them for testimonials.

My philosophy about email is a lot like the philosophy of "sustainable living." Every email should serve double, triple, even quadruple duty. Use it to build your writing habit, and warm up for the day's writing—but *also* use it to build your business and grow your reach. Think smart about email, and you'll discover that it's an amazing tool for success.

SAMPLE AUTORESPONDER SEQUENCE

This is a very basic version of what we just talked about. Feel free to add some real meat to these bones, and you can leverage them for your very first autoresponder sequence.

Email 1: Welcome!

SUBJECT: Welcome! Here's your fitness tip for Day 1!

Hi there!

I'm glad you've joined my list. Stay tuned, because for the next five days I'm going to give you some basic exercises and tips for staying fit in the office.

And here's your tip for Day 1!

Water is an essential part of life, so make sure you're drinking plenty of it. To make this a lot easier, fill a container, such as a spare pitcher, and keep it available for use throughout the day.

Cold water has actually been shown to help your burn calories, because your body has to expel heat to warm it. So if you have an insulated thermos or water bottle, fill it with ice water and sip it throughout the day!

That's today's tip, and there are four more on their way. Stay tuned! And thanks again for signing up!

Bob D. Builder

Fitness Expert

Email 2: Fitness Tip, Day 2

SUBJECT: Fitness Tip, Day 2!

Hi again!

Yesterday you signed up for the list, and I sent you the very first tip for staying fit in the office. Today's tip gets you out of your chair and on your feet!

Exercise is crucial for helping you get your brain in gear. So for today's tip, set a reminder on your computer's calendar or on your smartphone, and tell yourself to get up and take a lap around the office at least once every hour.

Just doing a quick lap, even if it's only a couple of minutes of walking, can get your blood pumping and make you feel more alert and ready to tackle your work. Combine this with drinking plenty of water, and you've got a winning combination for better heart health and quicker weight loss!

Tomorrow, you'll get another quick tip for fitness. But until then, have you seen my latest book, "The Office Workout Handbook?" It's available for sale right now on Amazon and other retailers, and it can be yours! <u>Click here to get your copy today!</u>

See you tomorrow for Day 3!

Bob D. Builder

Fitness Expert

You can see how this shapes up. Just keep adding to your sequence with something new and valuable for your reader, until you have a nice sequence that will engage them.

At the end of each email, try to include some kind of CTA that will help convert this free traffic into a paying customer. Offer your book or your course or anything else you have to sell. Be nice about it. Don't shove it in their face. Just make the offer, tell them how it benefits them, and then sign out. You'll have plenty of opportunities to "sell" as time goes by.

In the meantime, take advantage of this time. Creating autoresponders is good for your marketing, but it's also good for helping you develop your daily writing habit. Commit to doing a series in a specific amount of time. Commit to writing a specific number of words per email. And then follow through on the commitment by sitting down each day, at the same time, and knocking out an email per day.

I recommend doing it this way rather than knocking them all out at once. For starters, if you write a five-day email sequence then you have five days of coming back to the keyboard to do some writing. In addition, though, you'll also get a bit of the flavor your readers will get, when they start receiving your emails each day. You'll know the feel and the timing of all of them, and how they work together.

You won't regret this exercise, believe me. Combining writing autoresponders with writing daily blog posts will give you a set of practical and useful tools that will help you market yourself while also helping you develop your writing muscles.

PART 2 – 30-DAY AUTHOR PROCESS

CHAPTER 7
HOW TO WRITE A BOOK IN 30 DAYS (OR LESS)

By this point, you realize how important it is to actually sit down and write every day.

HINT: *Very* important.

Now, though, we need to trigger that muscle memory to do the one thing we really *want* to do with it—actually write a book.

There are few requirements for being an author, but one of them does happen to be "write a book." And writing book can be a tough task to take on. Believe me. I've done it a few times.

I wrote my very first book when was five years old—but that's just me showing off. Also, it's not like that book ever saw an audience beyond my parents, a few teachers, and my classmates. It did set a tone for my life, I believe. It established pretty early on that I was "the kid who writes." And I took that title and ran with it.

As of this writing, I have no fewer than 22 books available for purchase through Amazon, Apple's iBooks, Barnes & Noble, and thousands of book retailers worldwide. I primarily sell eBooks, but I have numerous paperbacks for sale as well.

And to date, I've taught or coached hundreds of authors in the craft and business of writing and publishing. I even broadcast to a whole audience of authors and will-be authors every week on my show, the Wordslinger Podcast (wordslingerpodcast.com) and on the Self Publishing Answers Podcast, which I co-host with authors Nick Thacker ("The Enigma Strain") and Justin Sloan ("Creative Writing Career").

When I talk to authors about this work, I tell them that they could have a book on the shelves within the next thirty days. And some of them actually believe me.

I think you're probably one of the believers. And if so, good on you. Because it's actually tough to believe, right? We've spent our whole lives being told how difficult it is to be an author, how difficult it is to write a book, and how we have to be prepared to spend months, even *years* toiling and writing before our work sees the light of day.

What if I told you that 30 days was actually kind of conservative?

Most of my first drafts take less than 15 days to write. I've actually written and published an entire book in just *five* days before. And I'm seriously considering trying to write and publish an entire book in just *one* day.

That all sounds wicked impressive, I know. But the truth is, it's just *math*.

There's a formula to all of this, and it isn't that difficult to work out.

We'll cover all this in the rest of this chapter. But before we get to *what* to do, let's take a look at what *not* to do.

HOW TO WRITE A BOOK IN 2+ YEARS

That first book I wrote, when I was five years old, took maybe a day to write. So … you know … *bow before me*.

But the next book I wrote took much longer. I penned it over the course of two years, working it into odd hours when I could, keeping at it until it was finished.

And it was *glorious*.

Not the book. The book was garbage. It was poorly constructed, and tended to ramble all over the place. The characters were flat and wooden, and the plot was virtually non-existent. But what *did* make it glorious was the fact that *I'd done it*. I'd actually written a book. A real, grown-up *book*.

Through a sad set of tragedies and circumstances, that first book never saw the light of day, and probably never will. But I *did* write it. And if I could do it once, I reasoned, then I could do it again.

It was a few years later before I tried again and actually succeeded. But again, it took nearly two years of wedging writing time between work and home life, heading to Starbucks on lunch breaks or getting up really early to spend a little time at the keyboard before heading to the office. It was a plodding, brutal sort of work, done during hours when I felt less like an author and more like a deluded moron obsessed with torturing himself.

It took forever.

But eventually, all plodding and torture complete, I had it—another completed book. And unlike that first one (or technically, the *second* one), it truly *was* glorious. It had all the right curves, if you know what I'm saying.

I'm saying it was well written, well plotted, and had great character development. What were *you* thinking?

Not only did I have it written, I also had a leg up on my younger self, in that I now knew how to edit, lay out, and publish my tome. I had a design background now, so I could design my cover and even do the book's layout. I had some editing experience, so I could clean up the draft (though, I admit, I should have gotten someone else to do this). In short, I could make this thing into real book (though I'd later revise just about everything about it, because I wasn't quite as advanced in all those things as I first thought).

Despite any flaws and foibles, I now had a book available for sale and adorning the shelves of readers and libraries alike.

It was the first book in a trilogy, and I was really gung-ho to get to the other books. I couldn't *wait* to knock those out!

Sort of ...

I mean, "couldn't wait" may be a bit strong.

The truth was, that first book took so much time, energy, and effort, it was enough just to see it hit distribution. I was *satisfied*. I could have retired from book writing for good at that point. Because writing another book was going to be *so freaking hard*.

I dreaded it. I was scared of it. Every time I thought about it, my stomach clenched and I wanted to vomit. And I could only *hope* that I would vomit up those other two books.

But I couldn't very well let it drop, now could I? I had promised a trilogy. And trilogies require three books, not just one.

So for another two years I slugged my way through Book 2. And in that time, I had lots of readers ask me where the next book was, when it was coming out, why I was taking so long. "Books take time," I said with a mock smirk that I figured might be read as a knowing confidence. But all the while I felt a gnawing guilt, because I knew the *real* reason that Book 2 wasn't already available was that I wasn't putting in the *time*.

After a huge two-year struggle, I finished the second book, much to the relief of both me and my readers. But again … I had promised a trilogy. So whatever good karma I may have garnered from finishing and publishing Book 2, it was quickly fading as Book 3 remained unwritten.

So the process started all over again. I had a third book to write, and it wasn't going to write itself. Damn the hideous thing.

Once again, the thought of spending another two years writing really put me off. It cost me another couple of years just in procrastination. Meaning that for two years, instead of trudging through Book 3, I spent all that potential writing time *dreading* the two years of writing time I'd have to spend. I did everything *but* write that book.

Your classic writer neurosis.

During all that time, and through all the emails and Facebook messages and personal pleadings of my readers, I had that gnawing guilt and anxiety eating away at me. At one point, I was dangerously close to deciding that I was going to quit. Forget Book 3. *Screw* Book

3. Book 3 can go to *hell*. I'm done. Who really wanted to be an author anyway?

Well ... *I* did. In fact, being an author was pretty much the only dream I had. It was the one thing I'd hung on to my entire life. It was the one thing I wanted more than *anything*. Could I really just walk away from it?

And then, in December 2013, it finally became too much.

I was either going to write this book or I had to hang it up, give up on the dream for good, and start focusing on something else entirely.

I couldn't bear the thought of walking out on it, though. My whole life, that dream of being an author was the one thing I could look back on as a consistent part of me. But how could I call myself an author if I couldn't finish what I'd started? I had to get this third book written.

That's when I decided that, if I was going to do this, I had to treat writing as a business. And that business required a product. And that product was *that stupid book*.

I needed a new approach. I needed advice, from people who had done what I was trying to do.

I started listening to podcasts, reading books, and sitting through tons of webinars and videos. Within months I had consumed tons of content about the business of writing, about developing writing habits, about honing my craft and getting past barriers and roadblocks. All that was inspiring and encouraging. And *none* of it wrote the book for me.

Surprise!

But what it *did* do was get me to start thinking about the business in the right way, and get me to start developing a daily writing habit that I could rely on.

When I had dipped my toe into this business before, I had written a few goals down. One of those was "find two hours a week to write."

Heh. That's cute.

Two *hours*? A *week*? That's like saying, "I want to be an Olympic gymnast, so I'm going to find two hours a week to practice."

I had to up my game on that. I had to start thinking in terms of daily targets, not wedged-in-moments. So, as I learned more about this business and about how other authors were doing it, I started to develop a method.

I started with a process almost identical to what I've given you in this book, so far. I wrote journal entries and blog posts, emails and affirmations. I got into the habit of sitting down every day, at the same time in the same place, and *writing*.

And then I finally started writing Book 3.

And it was *amazing*.

I committed to writing a set number of words each day, and I wouldn't let myself turn in for the evening until I had those words on the page.

I did that every day, coming back to the keyboard regardless of how I felt—uninspired or unenthused, or (sometimes) actually hyped up about it all. I came back, again and again. And I wrote. And I wrote. And I *wrote*.

And then I was done.

My goal had been to write fifty thousand words—the minimum length of a novel as established by Chris Baty as part of the guidelines for **National Novel Writing Month** (NaNoWriMo), and outlined in his book "No Plot? No Problem!" I set that goal, set a deadline (30 days), and determined how many words I would need to write each day to meet that goal.

On days when I was really on a roll, I might double, triple, or even *quadruple* my word target. Some days I even wrote *ten times* my daily word target. But there was never one single day in which I did not *at least* hit the word target. That was concrete. It was the Spice. It was Life.

The result of all that marching forth, regardless of what anxiety might plague me, was … interesting.

To be honest, I did not meet my goal. I did not write 50K words 30 days.

I wrote 70K words in 15 days.

Turns out, when you sit down and focus on doing something, a really *weird* thing happens: *Something gets done.*

I committed to the idea of writing 50K words within 30 days, and to do that I committed to writing a certain number of words per day. But as I wrote, it became easier to do. I was able to fly through page after page, until I had all the pages I needed for a book.

Was it perfect? Absolutely not. It required a lot of editing, which I had put off while I was doing the actual writing (which, it turns out, is a very good thing—more on this in a bit).

But here's something surprising—this book that I wrote in just 15 days needed *less editing* than the other two books I wrote over the span of *four years*.

Somehow, by turning off my internal editor and just focusing on meeting my daily word target, I was writing not only *faster* but *better*.

In addition, when I delivered the book to my readers, they *loved it*. They felt it was the stronger of the three. It had a cleaner voice, and a better pacing. It was remarkable work.

And that got me wondering: Could I do this again? Is this repeatable?

So I tried it.

I wrote another book in just 15 days. And then another. And then another.

At the end of about six weeks I had *four new books*. I *doubled* my previous output, and instead of it taking six years it took only *two months*.

During all of that, I was working to refine the process I used.

I switched from writing in Microsoft Word to writing in Scrivener, which I believe was a key component of my success.

I also created a formula—my **30-Day Writing Formula**—for determining my targets and goals. I used Scrivener's progress meter to track how I was doing, and I posted that progress live on my website and on Facebook for my readers to see. That meant **accountability**.

During that time, I was working full time as a Copywriter, and then as a Creative Director. I had major responsibilities. I had stress. But I stuck to my daily targets, and I made iterative and cumulative progress.

And you can too. You *will*, if you put this formula and process to work for you.

Let's take a look at the 30-Day Writing Formula, and see how it can help you write a book in 30 days (or less).

30-DAY WRITING FORMULA

Write a book in 30 days using my special, magic "sit your butt in a chair every day" formula:

$$TWT / TDC = TDT$$

Or in plain English ...

Total Word Target (TWT) divided by Target Days to Completion (TDC, aka "Deadline") = Total Daily Target (TDT)

You didn't know there'd be maths, did ya?

So if your TWT is 50K (a decent number of words to produce around 200 pages for a paperback book) and you know you want your TDC to be 30 days, then your TDT would be:

50,000 words / 30 days = 1,667 words per day

WANT YOUR WEEKENDS FREE?

If you only want to write on weekdays, that's going to skew things a bit, but it can still be done. Make your TDC 22 instead of 30 (because you're removing 8 weekend days).

So:

50,000 words / 22 days = 2,273 words per day

TRADE PAPERBACK

A typical page in a 6x9 trade paperback book has about 350 words. So we're talking about sitting down to write five or six pages per day.

I tell clients to split that word count up into increments of 1,500. So you can sit down first thing in the morning and write 1,500 words, then come back in the afternoon and write the other 1,000-ish words. In this way, the writing time is more manageable.

WRITING IN HALF THE TIME

By the way, if you can write that extra 500 words in the afternoon (making your daily total 3K), you'll actually **write your entire 50K book in just 16 days**.

So if you want to get your book done and in front of the reader even faster, commit to writing that 3K per day. It's not as tough as you might think—especially if you chunk it into multiple sessions.

THE KEY TAKEAWAY—MORE IS MORE

The great thing about this formula is that you can control exactly what your output will be. And the more words you drop onto a page in one sitting, the faster your book can get to market.

If you're a coach or a speaker, you may be able to repurpose some of your materials, such as a presentation or a an article or blog post you've written, and make this all happen even faster.

If you're a fiction author, it helps tremendously if you use story beats and outlines to figure out your plot beforehand. The better you know your story, the faster you can put words on the page.

And for non-fiction authors such as historians and biographers, you could also benefit from having everything mapped out before hand.

But in all truth—regardless of the type of writing you're doing, just the act of forcing yourself to hit a daily goal every day will get you really far. Even if you have to come back after the fact, and edit in (or out) some information, you're better off blazing through from beginning to end than spending hours, days, months, or years "contemplating."

The real power stroke here is to focus *only on the writing*.

TOTAL WORD TARGET FORMULA

We've been talking in terms of a 50K book, but that may not fit the word count you need. Some books may be less than 50K, and some may be more. How do you decide how many words your book needs to be?

Here's a simple formula (really more of a process) for figuring out your TWT:

STEP 1: Find three books that are similar to yours in content. You can take three books off of your shelves, or just browse three books at the library or book store.

STEP 2: Turn to a typical page in each book. This would be a page with no extra spaces inserted, such as you'd find at the beginning or end of a chapter, or on a page with a section break. You want a page full of text, from top to bottom.

STEP 3: Find a typical line from a typical paragraph. You can usually use the second line in any given paragraph. And notice, we're saying "line," not "sentence." You want a line of text that goes from the left margin to the right margin.

STEP 4: Count the number of words in this line.

STEP 5: Now count the number of lines on the page.

STEP 6: Multiply these two numbers together to get a typical word count for a typical page.

STEP 7: Multiply that number by the number of pages in the book.

STEP 8: Repeat the above steps for all three of your sample books.

STEP 9: Take your three numbers, add them together, and then divide by 3. This will give you the average word count for the three books, which you can use as your new Total Word Target (TWT).

YOU HAVE ONE JOB

You now have a process for figuring out exactly how much writing you need to do per day to meet your target goals. Once you've determined your TWT (total word target), you can choose any date range you like for your TDC (total days to completion). We've been talking in terms of 30 days, but you can go with more or with less, to taste.

Now that we know how many words to write per day, we can get to the **secret ingredient**.

What I'm about to impart to you is something that will change everything for you as an author. It may well be the greatest secret of the successful author—the ancient wisdom that is passed down from master to apprentice, generation after generation. This secret is so ground-shaking, so world-shaping, so career-making, I feel I must ask you to take a deep breath before reading it.

Ready? Phew. Here we go …

Turn off the internal editor.

Got it?

I know, I know. It doesn't seem like much, especially the build-up. But for all its simplicity, it packs a lot of *power*. Because it really is the secret to author success.

And most of the people reading this are going to ignore it.

This is a huge thing, a truly tall order, for a lot of authors—especially first-time authors. Because for many authors, it's all but *impossible* to turn off that inner editor and just focus on the writing and nothing else.

And it's ok. It's not your fault. You were *taught* to be this way.

In school, almost all of us were taught to approach writing as a very linear exercise, and one that required us to be focused and, dare I say, *perfect* in one stroke. We were given endless exams and essays in school, and told that we would be graded on content, accuracy, grammar and spelling, and completion. In effect, if we didn't get it perfect on the first try, we were screwed.

You poor, poor soul.

Because that is *not* the way a real author works.

Real authors *write*. That's what they do. In fact, writing is the *only* job an author has. Just the one.

Sounds insane, right?

But bear with me here.

If you waste time fussing over every word, or over getting every phrase *just right*, you'll never hit your daily targets. The system just can't handle that kind of perfectionism. You cannot, under any circumstances, worry about anything beyond the *one thing*: **Your job is to write**.

I repeat, you have *one job* during this process: You're writer, not an editor.

Later, you can be an editor. Today, you write.

Sound insane? It's not. It's actually the only sane thing you can do.

When you're writing a book, writing really is the only job you can handle. You aren't the book's marketer or cover designer or layout artist. You're not the printer or typesetter. You're not even the janitor. And you are certainly *not* the book's editor.

If you tried to do someone else's job in a company, you'd end up getting fired. That's because everyone in the company has their *own* job to do. They have their work, and you have yours.

Your own job would suffer, because you were too focused on the other guy's job. The other guy would resent you, and would undermine you every chance he got. And ultimately, you'd end up overworked and doing neither your job or his job very well.

So don't do that.

Do *your* job—which is to write.

And when you're *done* writing, *then* you can be the editor. And *that* will be your job.

Do an edit and a rewrite, to catch any obvious typos or gaffs or mistakes you might want to catch. That's separate time. Separate work.

And when you're done with that, **hire an editor.**

Pay someone *real money* to go through and polish your book. This isn't something you can cut corners on. This is your baby we're talking about. So do it right.

When you're writing—write.

When you're editing—edit.

When you're done, give it *someone else* to edit.

You'll be happier, you'll get the work done faster, and you'll end up with better work than you would have had otherwise.

CHAPTER 8
HOW TO CONQUER WRITER'S BLOCK

I'm going to be honest with you—I have no idea what "writer's block" really is. I have never experienced it. I can't describe it from a place of firsthand knowledge.

Sorry about that.

But I get this question from clients and other writers enough that I know it's something we need to address. So here goes ...

First, a standard definition:

> **Writer's Block—** n. the condition of being unable to think of what to write or how to proceed with writing.

Not very helpful, I know.

Look, all kidding aside, I do know what it's like to look at the page and panic because you have *no idea* what to write. It's just ... well ... that's never lasted more than a couple of seconds for me. Because after that, I just put my fingers to the keyboard and *started writing*.

Seth Godin sums up the idea of writer's block (and the cure for it) better than I can. So I steal from ... er ... *quote him* here:

TALKER'S BLOCK

No one ever gets talker's block. No one wakes up in the morning, discovers he has nothing to say and sits quietly, for days or weeks, until the muse hits, until the moment is right, until all the craziness in his life has died down.

Why then, is writer's block endemic?

The reason we don't get talker's block is that we're in the habit of talking without a lot of concern for whether or not our inane blather will come back to haunt us. Talk is cheap. Talk is ephemeral. Talk can be easily denied.

We talk poorly and then, eventually (or sometimes), we talk smart. We get better at talking precisely because we talk. We see what works and what doesn't, and if we're insightful, do more of what works. How can one get talker's block after all this practice?

Writer's block isn't hard to cure.

Just write poorly. Continue to write poorly, in public, until you can write better.

I believe that everyone should write in public. Get a blog. Or use Squidoo or Tumblr or a microblogging site. Use an alias if you like. Turn off comments, certainly—you don't need more criticism, you need more writing.

Do it every day. Every single day. Not a diary, not fiction, but analysis. Clear, crisp, honest writing about what you see in the world. Or want to see. Or teach (in writing). Tell us how to do something.

If you know you have to write something every single day, even a paragraph, you will improve your writing. If you're concerned with quality, of course, then not writing is not a problem, because zero is perfect and without defects. Shipping nothing is safe.

The second best thing to zero is something better than bad. So if you know you have to write tomorrow, your brain will start working on something better than bad. And then you'll inevitably redefine bad and tomorrow will be better than that. And on and on.

Write like you talk. Often.

SOURCE: Reprinted with permission. Copyright Seth Godin. http://sethgodin.typepad.com/seths_blog/2011/09/talkers-block.html

The thing about writer's block is that it's really just us feeling hesitation about our *start*. We feel afraid, maybe, because we *don't* know what to say or how to say it, and whatever does come out may be something people hate. It may be embarrassing. It may be *really bad*.

The good news is, that's what *editing* is for.

Writer's block is basically fear. And the only way to overcome fear is to *do something*. That's why it's so important to develop daily writing rituals, such as what we discussed in Part 1. Write affirmations. Write a journal entry. Write a blog post. Write *something*, so you can get the gears moving, get some kinetic energy in the mix, and then get to work.

If you're having trouble putting your ideas on the page, try putting them somewhere else first.

Chances are, you own a smartphone. Or a tablet. Or a laptop. Or maybe just a digital camera. You might even own a dedicated voice recorder. Each of those has a microphone, and each can record you simply *talking* about your topic. If you're having trouble *writing*, try *talking* for a bit, and then transcribe what you said.

It's slower. It takes a bit more effort. But it's a perfectly valid and handy way to go from the existential crisis of the blank page to actually having *words* on that page.

If talking to yourself doesn't do it, try talking to someone else. Enlist a partner. Have them ask you some questions, to get the ideas flowing. And then record and transcribe that conversation.

Use any trick you have to, but stick to your commitment to put words on the page every day. That, I promise, is the *only* way to truly beat writer's block once and for all. It's the only way to write a book or an email or anything else. Commit, and come back to the page every day until you've written what you're going to write.

10 TRICKS FOR BEATING WRITER'S BLOCK

If, despite your best efforts, you find yourself facing the blank page with no idea where to go with your writing, here are a few tricks that work. Try one, or try all. Or use them as inspiration for developing a trick of your own (and feel free to share that trick with me—go to kevintumlinson.com/contact to send me an email and tell me all about it!).

Talk it out — If you're having trouble getting started, grab your smartphone, tablet, or any other recording device and just start talking about your topic. If you're writing non-fiction, pretend you're describing your topic to someone who has never heard of it. If you're writing fiction, start by introducing your character, or (even better) have an actual *conversation* with your character, and see what he or she thinks and says. You'll be surprised.

Walk it out — Sometimes it helps to take a deep breath, stand up, walk out your front door, and just keep walking until you make the block. During that time, think about what you're trying to say. Pretend you're reading it aloud to a crowd, or maybe reading it on someone else's blog or in someone else's book. Imagine how it unfolds as if you weren't the one writing it, and then ... well ... *plagiarize* yourself.

Outline — Try writing your story in bullet form. Don't bother with numbers. Just start a bullet list and start detailing what happens next, and next, and next ...

Take a shower — Actually, it might be better to say "relax." Have you ever noticed how often a good idea comes when you're in the shower? That's mostly because you're relaxed, and you're letting your mind wander. Take advantage of that. When you find yourself stuck, go take a hot shower or bath, relax a bit, have some chamomile tea, listen to some soothing music. Keep a notepad or recorder nearby to capture your thoughts as they happen, but don't force them. Also, don't shower with your laptop or notepad. It won't end well.

Grab your partner — Sometimes it helps to have someone you can chat with about the writing. Call up your best friend or someone who knows what you're trying to do, and engage in some lively conversation on the topic. Brainstorm together, and you'll find yourself coming up with all kinds of ideas. You can always thank your buddy in the Acknowledgements of the book.

Read something off topic (or on topic) — Scan news headlines online and read something that catches your interest. Or pick up a book and read a chapter or two. Sometimes, just exposing yourself to language and ideas can be a great way to break the log jam in your brain and get you racing forward. I've found this works best if I'm reading something entirely unrelated to my topic, but I've also occasionally been inspired by research. Either way, reading is a writer's best habit, so dive in without hesitation.

Relocate — Sometimes your environment can get a little uninspiring. That's when it can help a lot to go find a new space. Go sit in a coffee shop or book store, or maybe an art museum. Personally, I love hotel lobbies—those grand, well-decorated areas in large hotels that typically have tables, coffee, and snatches of overheard conversation readily available. Some of my best work has come from the breakfast areas of hotels, where people are meeting and getting ready to venture out for activities and entertainment.

Decorate your space — You don't want your writing space to be a distraction … all the time. But it's good to get your brain out of the mud for a bit every now and then. Take some time to make your usual writing space into something filled with inspiration. I have a couple of cool prints on my walls—an artist rendering of the TARDIS from "Doctor Who," a blueprint of the Enterprise D from "Star Trek: The Next Generation," things like that. I also have a fine little collection of various scotches on a credenza near my desk, lots of old cameras, projectors, typewriters, and other visually interesting objects. These don't get in the way of my writing, but they can be nice to look at, and can sometimes inspire me to get moving. Try adding something interesting to your space and see what happens. You can always take it away if it turns out to be too distracting.

Coffee and snacks — Turns out, our brains are part of our bodies. And our bodies need fuel. If you're finding yourself spacing out as you stare at the page or screen, maybe you're just hungry. Have a small snack—maybe a small piece of chocolate. Coffee is also good, because it stimulates blood flow. And it's awesome. But if you're not into coffee, try a cup of tea (or, if you're from the South like me, a glass of iced tea). Red Bull is another favorite of mine, giving me just the right pep when I need it. If you can't do caffeine, even just sipping hot water with lemon can perk you up and get your brain in gear.

Listen to tunes — I've gone through all kinds of stages, when it comes to music playing while I write. When I'm in public, I just listen to whatever's going on the speakers overhead. On rare occasions that might be too distracting, so I'll plug in my earbuds and get my own playlist going. And that playlist can range from Funk to Celtic instrumentals to Christian contemporary to Blues to Motown. You just never know. But music has long been a cure for writer's block. It's inspirational and motivating. And, especially in today's culture, we're more or less trained to think of scenes in terms of music, so you may be inspired in your storytelling.

There are, of course, more than ten ways to combat writer's block. You know ... if you *believe* in that sort of thing. But these ten come from various other authors I've known and interviewed and just chatted with. And though I've never had writer's block, I've used some of these, if I ever felt like inspiration wasn't quite with me. So if you find yourself stuck at all, give one of these (or several of these) a try, and see what shakes loose.

CHAPTER 9
A TALE OF TWO EMAILS

Now that you have the daily writing habit and the formula for writing your book, let's take a moment to consider another aspect of writing that you'll find very useful: **Copywriting**.

A lot of my coaching and consulting clients have more than books on the brain. Many of them want to improve their copywriting skills as well. I give them the same process I just gave you, and walk them through all of it to help them get past any hurdles that may come up. One of those hurdles is almost universal—

"What do I *write* about?"

Believe it or not, if the plan is to write a book, I don't get this question quite as often. Not exactly.

Plenty of clients say they're stuck or stymied about what to write *next* …

"I've run out of ideas."

"I've covered everything I want to cover, and the book is only 5,000 words long!"

"I don't quite know how to say what I'm trying to say."

Those are common ailments for the will-be author, and each has to be dealt with on a case-by-case basis. Because—let's be honest here—I'm not the one who is most qualified to tell you *what to write*.

That would be *you*.

My job—my role in the coaching and consulting process—is to help you get past your hangups, to see things from a new perspective when you need to, and to nudge you to the answers you already have. I can't tell you what to write—I can only help you find it for yourself.

That's the way it works for writing books.

Copywriting, on the other hand ...

That's a slightly different game. Because unlike books, it's entirely possible to tell someone exactly what they should write when it comes to an email or an ad or a blog post. It all comes back to your message and your voice, the components of your brand that you're trying to express, the key benefit you're trying to deliver, and the call to action you want your reader to take.

Let's slow down and break that out, so that it's clear:

IN COPYWRITING, WHAT YOU WRITE COMES DOWN TO—

The key benefit—What pain point or problem are you solving, and how?

The value proposition—Why should readers trust you?

Branding, messaging, and voice—What is the "personality" you're trying to convey with what you're writing?

The call to action (CTA)—What action do you want your reader to take?

All good copywriting does everything on this list. It's what copywriting is *for*. And the more condensed the copy, the more noticeable and "in your face" each of these can be. If you have room to spread out, though, these components can practically disappear.

For example, if you're writing an email that's meant to promote a new piece of software your company is introducing, your copy might come down to a paragraph or two with a headline, body copy, and a CTA.

It might look like this:

> *Tired of keeping track of hundreds of passwords?*
>
> *KeySafe replaces all of your passwords with one simple keyword.*
>
> *Using NSA-level data encryption, KeySafe creates and stores unbreakable and uncrackable passwords for every site and application you use, and changes those passwords on a schedule you choose.*
>
> *You only have to remember one word, and it never changes. KeySafe does the rest.*
>
> *Try KeySafe for FREE for 15 days.*
>
> *You'll never need another password again.*

In this example, we open with the pain point: "Tired of keeping track of hundreds of passwords?"

We offer our solution: "KeySafe replaces all of your passwords with one simple keyword."

We offer the value proposition: "Using NSA-level encryption …" as well as "You'll never need another password again."

And we tell the reader what action to take: "Try KeySafe for FREE for 15 days."

Our entire copywriting strategy is compressed into just a couple of paragraphs. We know what to write, because we know our goals. We want to present a problem, then provide a solution, then provide an action for the reader to take.

If you're a novelist, your benefit statements and value propositions might look a little different, but you're still using the same process. The real difference is that you'll be a bit more overt and less circumspect in how you use the benefits and value propositions, but the call to action would be just as direct.

For example, the pain point might be: "The reader needs a good fantasy novel to provide entertainment."

The value proposition, then, would be something along the lines of: "I have a fantasy novel that is unique and fun to read."

The CTA, then, would be a variation on: "Buy and read my book to be entertained."

But to attract a fantasy reader, you have to dress all of this in more dramatic clothing.

That's where **branding and messaging** come in.

As an author, you have a "voice." Your work is written in a style and tone, and so your marketing communications need to reflect that. Stick to a tone that matches what you've written in your book.

So for a fantasy novel, you might write:

> *Braverman has only three sunsets to turn back eternal darkness.*
>
> *A curse covers the land, taking the sight from everyone it touches. It strikes in the night, and brings with it both blindness and a pain like fire in the blood. In three nights, the curse will swallow all of humanity, cursing every living soul to eternal darkness and unending pain.*
>
> *Braverman is the forgotten heir—the bastard son of an uncaring king. But as the curse destroys the royal family, Braverman learns that only his untainted royal blood can save the world. He alone can enter the Citadel of Light, and break this curse of darkness before it claims every living soul.*
>
> *But the Dark Enemy knows Braverman well. She gave birth to him, after all.*
>
> *In three days the world falls into eternal darkness—see it while you can.*
>
> *Read BLOOD CURSE today!*
>
> *Available in paperback and eBook.*

You'll notice that this email is a bit longer than the previous one. We needed a bit more room to build the drama and entice the reader. And that's ok. Our goal is to be concise, but it also has to be effective. As long as we avoid writing another book just to promote the first, we're largely ok.

The important thing is that we captured all of the key components of good copywriting in this email, even with all the drama.

The headline offers a pain point: "Braverman has only three sunsets to turn back eternal darkness."

That's pretty potent. The pain for our reader is, "Why does Braverman only have three sunsets? How will he do it?!?"

In other words, the pain point is the tension we created by introducing the story in an enigmatic way. We enticed the reader to read further by posing an unusual and dramatic scenario, and their "pain" becomes their need to know what happens next.

The solution we offer is where things vary just a bit form the non-fiction counterpart.

Our solution, in this case, is to tease more of the story. We explain a bit more about the headline in the paragraphs that follow. We give some background on Braverman and the kingdom and the curse. And then we tease the audience a bit more by revealing that the antagonist in the story is Braverman's mother. Oooooh! Chills!

That's our value proposition. Did you catch it?

Where the value prop in the non-fiction email was about how our software solves their password problems, the value prop in this email is how our story will answer questions raised in this pitch, and how we'll pay off all of this drama and tension we've created. Our value prop, in other words, is our unspoken promise that if the reader buys the book, they'll be entertained.

The call to action is as straightforward as it gets. "Read BLOOD CURSE today!" Buy the book. Read the book. Do it today.

You can see how knowing what pain you're solving and how you solve it can help you determine what to write in an email or an ad. Point out a problem, offer a solution, give a call to action.

So how does this relate to writing a book in 30 days?

It's mostly about the marketing, to be honest. And marketing is something every author, 30-Day variety or otherwise, needs to think about.

But beyond that, the tricks used to write a marketing email for your book will also come in handy for writing the book's description for its sales page or back cover. It's the **pitch** of your book—the thing that will inspire readers to actually *be* readers.

It's also a good way for you to sum up what you're writing before you start. If you find yourself stuck for "what to write next," try writing one of these pitches, or referring back to one you wrote earlier, and see if that helps nudge you to the next step.

Keep in mind that your goal as a writer is to provide something useful to your reader. You want to solve a problem. You want to reduce a pain. It's a good idea for you to know exactly how you're going to do that.

CHAPTER 10
WHAT TO DO ONCE YOUR BOOK IS WRITTEN

So there it is.

Nothing held back, and all cards on the table. The entire "secret" to writing a book in 30 days or less.

By this point, you (hopefully) have developed a daily writing habit that will take you far, young Padawan. That's good—because writing daily means improving fast. And if you take nothing else at all form this book, the idea of a daily writing habit is probably the best thing you can latch on to.

There are basically two essential habits a writer needs to nurture daily: Reading and writing.

My best advice to you is read wide and read often, and write every single day. Even if all you write is a quick email to a co-worker or a thank-you note to a friend, write *something*. And while you're writing, do your best to make it the best writing you've ever done. Every bit of practice builds muscle you'll rely on when you need it in the future.

Now that you've read through the 30-Day Writing formula and the various techniques, you hopefully have a plan in place for tackling your topic or your story, and getting it out of your head and onto the page. That's really what this all comes down to—**developing a habit, creating a plan, and working the plan**.

So what happens once you've worked that plan and you've produced a draft of your book?

Now we get into a whole new world.

In many respects, what happens *after* writing a book could be a book in itself. There are so many options and variables and strategies, I won't be able to cover all of them in this book. But I can give you an overview and a basic strategy for how to take your book from draft to bookshelves (physical or digital).

Here are a few tips that will help ...

EDITING

Remember earlier when I told you that you only have *one job* as a writer—to write? That's still true. Your job as a writer is to write. But when the writing is done, you can pull on your Editor's CapTM and take on a whole new role in your project.

Editing is as much a talent and skill as writing. In fact, in a lot of ways editing may actually require *more* talent and skill than writing—because while you can "pants" or improvise your way through writing a book, editing requires you to slow down, think strategically, and to sometimes make hard decisions about the work.

To be honest, editing isn't for everyone.

For instance—I'm not a very good editor. In fact, I kind of stink at it. I'm too impatient, and too forgiving of my own flaws. I'm not detail oriented, so the subtle errors escape me.

Don't get me wrong—I *can* edit, and I do. I'm very good at spotting awkward phrasing and cleaning up language to make it more concise and more efficient. But spotting every little typo and grammar gaff? Hardly. I'm better off handing the work to the pros.

That's what I recommend for you, too.

In fact, I recommend it, even if you're a master at editing yourself. Because, frankly, no matter how good you are, you are going to miss things in your own work that you might have caught in someone else's.

If you are on a tight budget, hiring an editor might seem a bit daunting. It really can be pricey. But if you're serious about writing as a business, it's worth the expense. A good editor can mean the difference between a book your family thinks is really neat and a book that's being optioned for motion picture rights.

That said, it would be a shame to have to bust the piggy bank open for an editor, if there was an alternative.

Here are a few suggestions that might help:

Use beta readers—One of the best things about being a writer is the readers. If people like what you're writing, they'll do just about anything to help you write more of it, and get better at it.

I love my readers. *LOVE* them. You should too. And if you love them right, you can ask them to help you work the kinks out of your manuscript.

If you don't already have a list of beta readers to call on, you can start building one by utilizing the tools you already have. Use your blog and social media platforms to attract readers to your work, and then offer them a free peek at your latest work if they'll agree to point out any typos or gaffs. In marketing parlance, we call this a "street team," or an "advanced team." These are your first line of defense against the perils of typoism.

Ask your groups—You can also turn to people in any writing or mastermind groups you belong to, and offer to let them have an exclusive first look at your book if they'll help you spot any errors. The key here is to cultivate a mutually beneficial relationship with the people in your group. Be friends. Be open to reading *their* work, and giving good feedback. Like any relationship, this one will need some maintenance. There will be (*must be*) some give and take.

Be courteous, offer something in return, and be open to honest feedback and edits when someone agrees to take on your manuscript.

Find an up-and-comer—Sometimes you just can't avoid paying *something* for editing. But to minimize your out of pocket expenses, you could try finding an editor who is trying to establish him- or herself in the business. Services like Upwork (formerly oDesk and Elance) are good sources for finding these folks. You could also try Fiverr.com, which has actually led me to a few really good editors from time to time (though they require a bit more vetting).

You could also go to a local college or university and ask someone in the English department if they could point out a would-be editor. College students often need money for necessities—however they define them—and you could end up starting a very good long-term editor/writer relationship with someone if you could throw them a few bucks in their time of "need."

Your results may vary with any given one of these approaches, but between your own editing and the help of an outsider, you'll probably do just fine.

In fact, if you want to increase your odds a bit, you could double up on a few of these. Get a handful of beta readers to each give you their feedback, make the edits, and then hire someone from Upwork or Fiverr to give it another pass for a few bucks. After half a dozen people have put eyes to your book, you've probably caught the majority of what needs to be caught.

SELF-EDITING TRICKS

You can, of course, edit yourself.

In fact, you should. Just not *exclusively*. Your editing is really just an extension of the writing and polishing process. Bringing in an outsider will help you catch the things you missed.

When you're self editing, there are a few "tricks" you can use to make things more efficient, and to catch more goofs.

Read it backwards—This is one of the oldest editing tricks in the world, but it's ridiculously effective. Start from the end of your book, and the last word of a sentence, and go through it word by word. It's time consuming, and a little labor intensive, but you'll catch tons of spelling errors and typos this way.

Use a ruler—Actually, any straight edge will work. Use a piece of paper or a credit card, or anything that helps you home in and focus on just the sentence you're reading. I recommend doing this along with reading it backwards, going sentence by sentence from end to beginning. By taking the sentences out of context, you're able to concentrate on just that sentence, it's meaning, and anything that might be amiss.

Read out loud—This is a favorite of a lot of writers. Read your book aloud and record as you go. You'll spot flaws much easier, and you'll also catch awkward phrasing or word choice. Plus, as a bonus you could technically edit that audio into an audiobook version of your book, if you were so inclined (and if the quality is high enough).

Another version of this technique is to read the book to a partner, or have them read it to you. We're usually much better at hearing flaws when someone else is speaking or reading. It's a human thing.

Chunk it—One of the things that makes editing difficult for some people is the sheer volume of what they have to get through. After all, you just *wrote* this book. Now you have to read it *again?*

So one technique that can help is to chunk the work similar to the way we chunked the writing. Break the book into several parts—you can use chapters, if you like, but I'd recommend getting even more granular, maybe down to scenes or sections if you can. Find a daily target you can work to. Maybe you commit to editing four pages per day, for instance. Do that every day and you'll get through the whole book in good time. It will dampen some of the anxiety and the feeling of being overwhelmed by the work, and it will help you be more efficient in the process

Use any or all of these techniques in any configuration you like. The more times you go back to edit, the more readily you'll find errors and omissions.

And once you've done your edits, hand the work off to another editor and have them do the same. Don't rely on your editing alone—it won't end well.

Editing is kind of a pain, but it's a vital and necessary part of the writing process. For some writers, this is where the *real* writing actually happens. It can be the time during which you figure out what your book really is, and what it can be. So take this step seriously. Bring in help. Do it right.

LAYOUT

My first book was laid out in Microsoft Word, and it was a *nightmare*.

I spent weeks fiddling with it to get it right. I somehow kept screwing everything up, and the headers would get completely janky. Section breaks would come in the middle of a paragraph. Page numbers would start over at "1" after every chapter, unless they were starting with "x."

I learned how to use Adobe InDesign just so I could have more control over layout. But even that has its challenges. For starters, it's a behemoth of a program to learn. And, as accustomed as I was to the awesomeness that is Photoshop, I found it frustrating that most of the keyboard shortcuts I used regularly were mapped to something entirely different in InDesign.

I briefly tried my hand at LaTex—an open source typesetting software you can download for free online. It had its merits. But I found it equally difficult to learn, and I ended up abandoning it and going back to InDesign.

Later, I discovered that Scrivener has some powerful layout tools, especially for eBooks. In fact, every eBook I publish comes more or less straight out of Scrivener's compile tool. That's been incredibly helpful, taking hours out of my old process of tweaking layout for the various eBook platforms.

But there were still the print books.

I'm much better with InDesign now, but it still, occasionally, takes a great deal of time. So on a whim, I recently decided to give MS Word another go. I downloaded a template I found online, and used that to do the layout of my second *Sawyer Jackson* book.

I was thrilled with the result.

I won't kid you—there are serious perks to using a professional layout suite. But for most books, you can get away with using MS Word or even Apple Pages to give you a pretty impressive layout. You can control fonts, header styles, and a lot of other factors that make a big difference in the professional look and feel of your book.

I've modified that original template, and I offer it on my site at kevintumlinson.com/resources. Go grab that, and see how it works for you.

BUT FOR THE NON-DIY CROWD ...

Doing it yourself isn't always the best plan, especially when it comes to something as crucial as the layout and formatting of your book. There are nuances to layout that are difficult to wrap your head around. And seemingly insignificant quirks can lead to huge headaches and even existential nightmares later. There's nothing quite like reviewing a digital or (worse) printed proof copy of your book just to discover that a quarter of it is in *italics and underlined*.

That happened to me on the 700+ page compilation of my *Citadel* series, and it took quite a bit of fiddling to figure out why it was happening, and to fix it.

So unless you're already somewhat familiar with layout and professional printing, you might consider outsourcing this part of your book to someone else. It's true, it can be a little pricey to pay someone to do the layout of your book. But it can shave weeks off of the delivery time, and will be worth it if you can afford it.

Layout designers are actually pretty easy to find. Go to Upwork or Fiver and you'll come across tons of designers who can give your book a full pro treatment. Your cost will vary by designer, but I recommend finding someone who knows what they're doing and has a decent track record. Ask to see some examples of layouts they've done, and make your decision based on the quality of work as much as on the price.

If you're having trouble finding a layout designer, you can ask me for one. I know tons of designers, and have worked with many of them for years. Contact me at kevintumlinson.com/contact to ask for a suggestion and I'll be happy to point the way.

COVER DESIGN

In the same vein as editing and layout, cover design is one of those tricky things you might just consider outsourcing from the start. In fact, unless you have some serious design skills—more than just knowing the basics of Photoshop—I just flat-out recommend you go elsewhere for your cover.

This isn't just about the actual *design* of your cover, by the way. There's actually a psychology to cover design that you should take into account. There are marketing considerations to make, and design theory and consumer theory to consider. Seriously— this can make or break you as an author.

That said—I know that a lot of people are going to try to design their own cover anyway. I mean, seriously ... "how hard could it be?"

Here's the thing ... you remember the first time you learned to drive a car? You'd seen cars driven for years. You watched your parents do it. You may have even watched your siblings or some friends do it. You watched movies, you watched TV. You had a racing game that was *incredibly realistic*. So driving should have been a snap.

But that first lesson went so *wrong*, didn't it? You stopped and started randomly. You had trouble balancing the motion between the gas pedal and the brake pedal. You had no idea what all those letters on the shifter meant. It was a mess.

There's always more to these things than you expect.

You certainly *can* learn to design a cover, and to do it well. But it isn't something that you'll pick up right away. Remember, it took more than one lesson to learn to drive. You had to get a few things wrong before you finally got it right.

With your cover, you really can't afford to get it wrong.

Covers are important. *Really* important. Consider the two covers below:

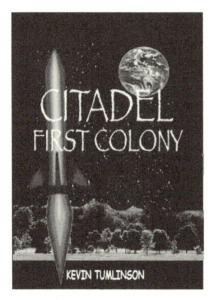 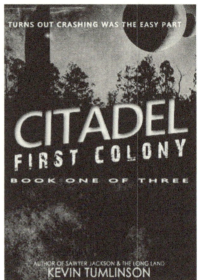

I have to confess: I made both of these covers. The one on the right I designed several months ago in an effort to optimize and improve my earlier covers—which weren't *bad*, but weren't quite right for my market.

The one on the left, however, I made about ten minutes ago. It's never been seen by eyes other than yours. Thank God. It was thrown together using whatever images I could find, and using the most basic tools in Photoshop.

So here's the deal—you should be able to see the *universe* of difference between these two covers. The one on the left is thrown together using clip art and some hastily edited images, while the one on the right has been built around a *strategy*. It has had a lot of thought applied to it in terms of composition, readability, and reliability to the genre.

The thing is, the cover on the left is actually more common from first-time indie authors. In fact, there's a good chance that someone is looking at this image right now and wondering, "What's so wrong with that?"

And that's exactly why you're better off going with a professional to design your cover. Because either A) your skills are only at the level where you could produce the cover on the left, or B) you don't even realize that the cover on the left is offensive to the sensibilities of both man and beast.

Or, you may be among those rare few who are actually good at this part. And if that's the case, go for it. You'll certainly save some cash. But consider—just for a moment—whether you're *actually* good at this, or just really, really want to *believe* you are.

There's a reason I redesigned my cover to optimize it. I designed the very first cover for this book, and then a second, and then a third. The version you see on the right is actually the *fourth* version of this cover to come from my hands.

I took the long way around.

And, in many respects, I think it may have cost me. During a time when self published authors were getting a bad rap for poor cover design, mine was actually a cut above. But it didn't feel like a pro cover. It had flaws. And those flaws may have turned off early potential readers.

I feel confident in this cover now, but that confidence came only after gaining a *lot* of experience.

I was a Creative Director for a time, and I've worked in marketing and advertising for decades. I've worked closely with hundreds of designers, and I've directed a lot of creative work. So now, I'm seeing things I did not see before. I still make mistakes, but I'm likely more qualified to take the risk than most indie authors.

If you are considering designing your own cover to save on the cost of hiring someone, just do yourself a favor and get lots of outside opinions and advice. Go find covers that work, and are professionally designed, and try your best to imitate the style. That will help.

But you probably be better off having your cover designed by someone else.

OUTSOURCING A COVER

There are many ways to get your cover designed by someone else, and some of them may actually be quite economical.

First, I absolutely have to recommend ReadyCovers.com.

I have to … because I'm one of the owners of it. So … full disclosure and all that.

But the point of ReadyCovers.com is to build a community for designers and authors to interact. There are pre-built covers available for purchase, and some may actually inspire your work. You can pay for the cover and have the artist edit the text for you. Bam. Done.

You can also connect with a designer you like, and have them build you a custom cover. This will be a bit pricier, but it may be worth it. You get a unique cover, tailored to your taste, and you make contact with a designer you may work with for years to come.

That's the plug for ReadyCovers, but I'd be a pretty crappy author if the only choice I gave you was the one I owned. So …

Additional options include 99 Designs, which is an incredibly popular and useful environment for finding graphic designers. With this service you can actually run a contest that lets you submit the concept of your book and get art concepts from hundreds of designers. You can have friends and family vote on the covers they like best, and you only pay for the cover you choose. It's a fantastic way to get high-end, professional cover design at an affordable price. Go to kevintumlinson.com/resources and click on the 99 Designs link to get started today.

Other services, such as Fiverr.com or Upwork.com, can also provide you with designers who can do the work for you. But buyer beware—often, the work you get from Fiverr.com is pretty shoddy, and often not even worth the five bucks.

Upwork can actually provide you with an amazing designer, but it may also cost you more out of pocket. And finding a good designer can sometimes be a time-consuming chore.

Of all the options, you'll just have to pick the one that works best for you. But I do encourage you to use a service and a professional, rather than trying to design your cover on your own. The results will almost always be better.

MOSTLY THE END

That pretty much takes care of everything you really need to know in order to be a **30-Day Author**. And by now, you've probably figured out that the title of this book is a bit misleading.

Because the truth is, you can be a 30-Day Author, or a 15-Day Author, or a 300-Day Author. The timing is entirely up to you. The process here is more about finding your rhythm, finding your groove, and developing a repeatable, reliable, and predictable system for churning out books any time you want. The number of days doesn't matter quite as much as the system itself.

When I talk to people about this program, I'm always amazed that no one stands up and says, "What? That's it? Put my butt in the chair every day? I could have thought of *that*!"

And it's true. Anyone could have thought of it. This isn't exactly new stuff. It's old. *Really* old.

The thing is, no one *does* think of it, most of the time. They get too hung up on some weird, fantasized version of what it means to be an author, and they get off track. They forget about the principle of "work hard, and be consistent," and they somehow get into this frame of mind that being an author means doing things in a *particular way*. You have to have a pipe and a smoker's jacket. You have to live in a shack, surrounded by goats. You have to drink scotch.

Ok, that last one actually is a requirement.

But the truth is, being an author is really just about perseverance and planning. And enough of one may actually compensate for a lack in the other.

I hope you got something important out of this book. I really do. It was something of a labor of love to write, and I was happy to do it. But here's a true confession for you: I didn't write this book in 30 days.

Actually, chunks of this book were written here and there over the course of the past year. I started doing the 30-Day Author talks to small groups about a year ago, and from those I developed several handouts, blog posts, articles, and booklets. And all of that material eventually piled up, and started beckoning to me.

"Write me," it said. "Hey bro ... write me."

So I did.

Most of what you just read came from all those various touch points over the course of a year. About 15,000 words of it, at any rate. The remaining six thousand or so words? Those came from today.

In other words, if we're going to be all technical about it, I actually wrote this entire book in *one day*.

Depending on how you look at it.

I'm telling you all of this to make a point:

BOOKS AREN'T WHAT YOU THINK THEY ARE.

Seth Godin has said something to this effect. He says that books aren't books anymore. Not the way we've always thought of them. Books, now, can be just about anything we can imagine. In fact, physical books, the paperback and hardback kind, are more often considered *souvenirs*. They're that thing an author signs, when the reader wants something tangle to hold on to.

Chances are you probably have a ton of material just laying around, ready to be pulled together into a book. Blog posts, pamphlets, notes, presentations—there's probably a lot of that stuff on your hard drive.

For fiction writers, you may have a ton of short stories sitting and waiting to be "done with." Have you considered taking a handful of those, editing them, getting covers for them, and putting them on Amazon to sell as novellas? You'd be surprised how popular those can be. And they go a long way toward helping you build a reputation and credibility as an author.

Don't get hung up on semantics. Decide that you're an author, and then go out and produce the book that works best for you definition. Use the strategies in this book to get yourself on track. Write every single day. And produce books, dammit. Produce them like the wind.

RESOURCES FOR THE 30-DAY AUTHOR

If you find yourself in need of some tools to make this stuff go, I have a great list for you.

Slip over to kevintumlinson.com/resources. You'll find a ton of links there, and the list grows all the time. It's not just a writer's resource—I have links for everything from tools to gadgets to books I think are great. You may be surprised. But all of it is cool. And there are plenty of writer resources there.

While you're there, sign up on my mailing list, and get three of my best books for free. You can do that right on the resources page, or you can go to kevintumlinson.com/starterlibrary.

Good luck in your 30-Day Author journey!

STUFF AT THE END OF THE BOOK

This book was the product of a lot of conversations, blog posts, articles, and random ideas, talked over with friends. Usually while consuming coffee, scotch, or both.

At the end of most of my books these days, I like to do these "Stuff at the End of the Book" articles. They're a good way to get some of the behind the scenes stuff out there, to show how the sausage is made, in effect. But this time around, the whole *book* is more or less "behind the scenes."

So I thought I'd take this time, and this space, to send you a very important message:

You are not alone.

Writing can be a lonely business. It can mean long hours hunched over keyboards or notebooks, all by your lonesome, in quiet hours of the day or night. It can mean turning your back on the obvious fun and shenanigans of your friends and family. It can mean brooding over ideas for long hours. But all of that does not have to be done in a vacuum.

If you're finding yourself in need of someone to bounce ideas off of, or to talk with about your work, then I encourage you to join the conversation on my author page on Facebook:

https://www.facebook.com/jkevintumlinson

There will be folks there that you'll be able to pal around with, share you work with, share your woes with. And your victories, because you'll have those too.

See you there.

HOW TO MAKE AN AUTHOR STUPID GRATEFUL

If you loved this book, and you'd like to see more like it, I can totally help with that. And there are some things you can do that will help *me* help *you*.

(1) REVIEW THIS BOOK

Go to Amazon, Goodreads, Apple's iBook store and anywhere else you can think of and leave a review for this book. Seriously—**I can't tell you enough how much this helps!**

The more reviews a book has, the more discoverable it becomes. Help me build and grow an audience for the books so I can keep writing and publishing them!

(2) BECOME A SLINGER

Slingers are what I call the people who are on my mailing list. They get the latest updates on new book releases, blog posts, podcast episodes, and (coolest of all) FREE GIVEAWAYS.

Best of all, if you sign up, you can get the Kevin Tumlinson Starter Library for FREE.

Go to http://kevintumlinson.com/starter-library-cta to download your free books now!

(3) TELL YOUR FRIENDS

Without readers, an author is just some guy with a really crappy hobby. Long hours at the keyboard. Tons of money spent on editing, layout, cover design. Even more long hours waiting for reviews and sales and bits of praise on Twitter. Honestly, a fella could take up fishing.

So please, spread the word. If you liked this book, tell a friend. Send them to that link above and let them download some free books. Help me grow this author business, and I promise I'll do everything I can to keep you entertained as much as possible!

Thanks for your help. And thanks for reading.

Kevin Tumlinson

ALSO BY KEVIN TUMLINSON

Citadel
Citadel: First Colony
Citadel: Paths in Darkness
Citadel: Children of Light Citadel: Omnibus
Citadel: The Value of War

Sawyer Jackson
Sawyer Jackson and the Long Land
Sawyer Jackson and the Shadow Strait

Wordslinger
30-Day Author: Develop A Daily Writing Habit and Write Your Book In 30 Days (Or Less)

Standalone
Getting Gone
Teresa's Monster
The Three Reasons to Avoid Being Punched in the Face
Tin Man
Two Blocks East
Edge
Evergreen

Watch for more at kevintumlinson.com

Made in the USA
Coppell, TX
11 August 2021